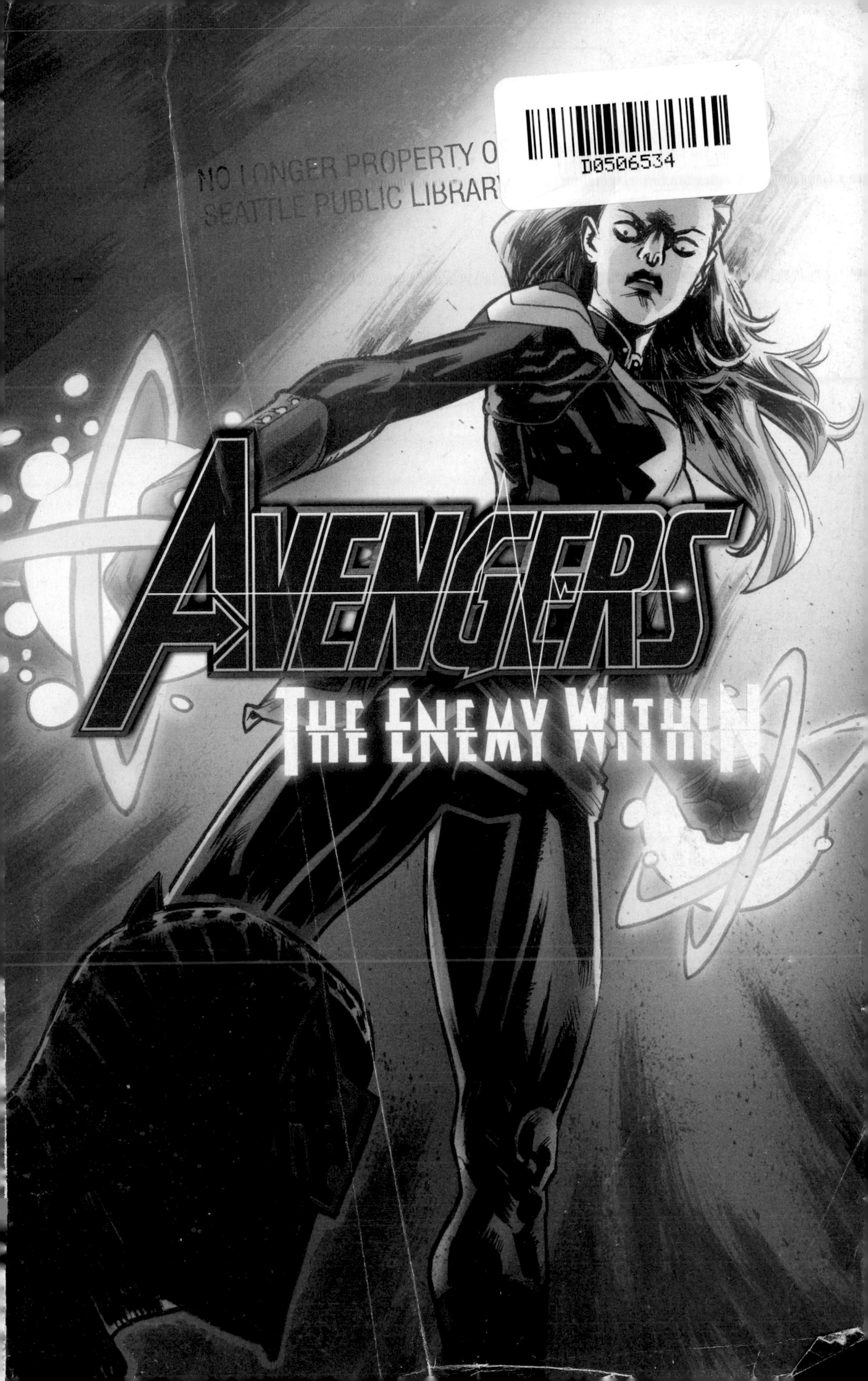
AVENGERS
THE ENEMY WITHIN

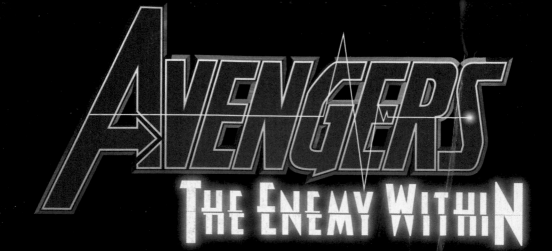

AVENGERS
THE ENEMY WITHIN

WRITER
KELLY SUE DeCONNICK

AVENGERS: THE ENEMY WITHIN #1
ARTIST
SCOTT HEPBURN

COLOR ARTIST
JORDIE BELLAIRE

LETTERER
VC'S JOE CARAMAGNA

AVENGERS ASSEMBLE #16-17
ARTIST
MATTEO BUFFAGNI
WITH **PEPE LARRAZ** (#17)

COLOR ARTIST
JORDIE BELLAIRE
WITH **MATTHEW WILSON** (#16)
& **NOLAN WOODARD** (#17)

LETTERER
VC'S CLAYTON COWLES

CAPTAIN MARVEL #13-14
ARTIST
SCOTT HEPBURN
WITH **GERARDO SANDOVAL**

COLOR ARTISTS
JORDIE BELLAIRE
& **ANDY TROY**

LETTERER
VC'S JOE CARAMAGNA

CAPTAIN MARVEL #17
ARTIST
FILIPE ANDRADE

COLOR ARTIST
JORDIE BELLAIRE

LETTERER
VC'S JOE CARAMAGNA

COVER ARTIST
JOE QUINONES

ASSISTANT EDITORS
JAKE THOMAS & DEVIN LEWIS

ASSOCIATE EDITOR
TOM BRENNAN

EDITORS
SANA AMANAT & LAUREN SANKOVITCH

SENIOR EDITOR
STEPHEN WACKER

EXECUTIVE EDITOR
TOM BREVOORT

Collection Editor: Cory Levine • Assistant Editors: Alex Starbuck & Nelson Ribeiro
Editors, Special Projects: Jennifer Grünwald & Mark D. Beazley • Senior Editor, Special Projects: Jeff Youngquist
SVP of Print & Digital Publishing Sales: David Gabriel • Book Design: Jeff Powell

Editor in Chief: Axel Alonso • Chief Creative Officer: Joe Quesada
Publisher: Dan Buckley • Executive Producer: Alan Fine

AVENGERS: THE ENEMY WITHIN. Contains material originally published in magazine form as AVENGERS: THE ENEMY WITHIN #1, CAPTAIN MARVEL #13-14 and #17, and AVENGERS ASSEMBLE #16-17. First printing 2013. ISBN# 978-0-7851-8403-4. Published by MARVEL WORLDWIDE, INC., a subsidiary of MARVEL ENTERTAINMENT, LLC. OFFICE OF PUBLICATION. 135 West 50th Street, New York, NY 10020. Copyright © 2013 Marvel Characters, Inc. All rights reserved. All characters featured in this issue and the distinctive names and likenesses thereof, and all related indicia are trademarks of Marvel Characters, Inc. No similarity between any of the names, characters, persons, and/or institutions in this magazine with those of any living or dead person or institution is intended, and any such similarity which may exist is purely coincidental. **Printed in the U.S.A.** ALAN FINE, EVP - Office of the President, Marvel Worldwide, Inc. and EVP & CMO Marvel Characters B.V.; DAN BUCKLEY, Publisher & President - Print, Animation & Digital Divisions; JOE QUESADA, Chief Creative Officer; TOM BREVOORT, SVP of Publishing; DAVID BOGART, SVP of Operations & Procurement, Publishing; C.B. CEBULSKI, SVP of Creator & Content Development; DAVID GABRIEL, SVP of Print & Digital Publishing Sales; JIM O'KEEFE, VP of Operations & Logistics; DAN CARR, Executive Director of Publishing Technology; SUSAN CRESPI, Editorial Operations Manager; ALEX MORALES, Publishing Operations Manager; STAN LEE, Chairman Emeritus. For information regarding advertising in Marvel Comics or on Marvel.com, please contact Niza Disla, Director of Marvel Partnerships, at ndisla@marvel.com. For Marvel subscription inquiries, please call 800-217-9158. **Manufactured between 10/11/2013 and 11/18/2013 by QUAD/GRAPHICS, VERSAILLES, KY, USA.**

10 9 8 7 6 5 4 3 2 1

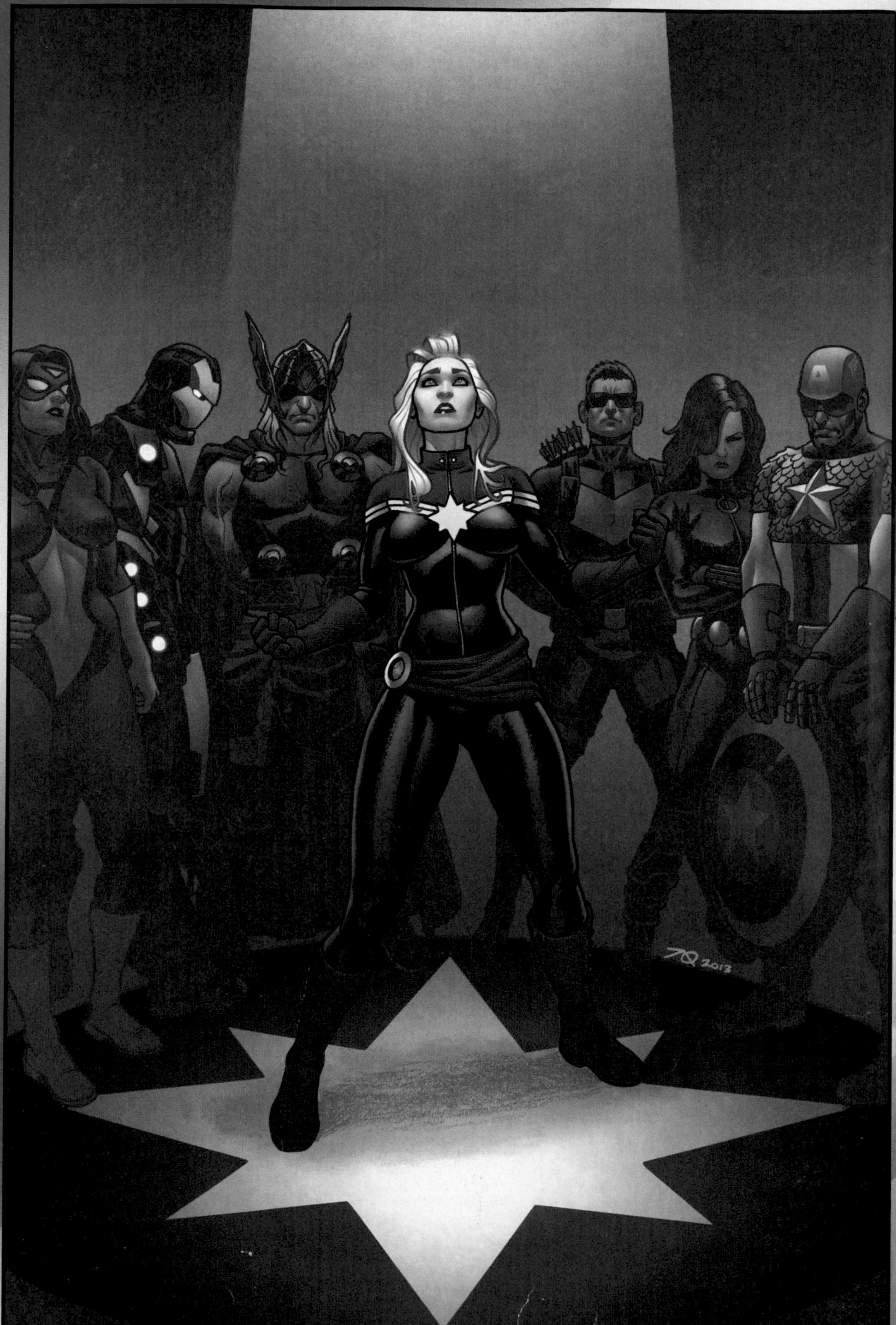

AVENGERS: THE ENEMY WITHIN #1

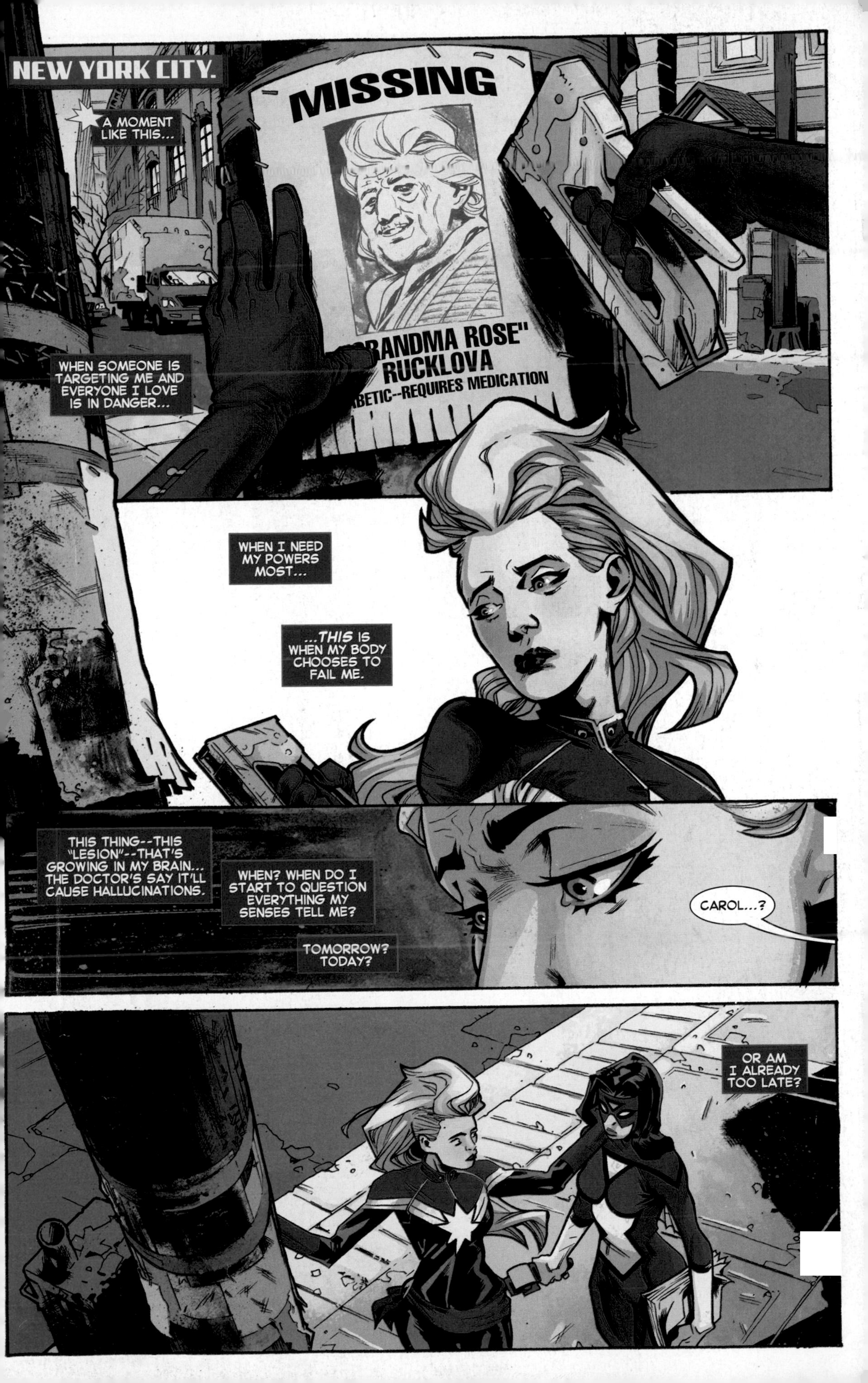
NEW YORK CITY.
A MOMENT LIKE THIS...
MISSING
"GRANDMA ROSE" RUCKLOVA
BETIC--REQUIRES MEDICATION
WHEN SOMEONE IS TARGETING ME AND EVERYONE I LOVE IS IN DANGER...
WHEN I NEED MY POWERS MOST...
...THIS IS WHEN MY BODY CHOOSES TO FAIL ME.
THIS THING--THIS "LESION"--THAT'S GROWING IN MY BRAIN... THE DOCTOR'S SAY IT'LL CAUSE HALLUCINATIONS.
WHEN? WHEN DO I START TO QUESTION EVERYTHING MY SENSES TELL ME?
TOMORROW? TODAY?
CAROL...?
OR AM I ALREADY TOO LATE?

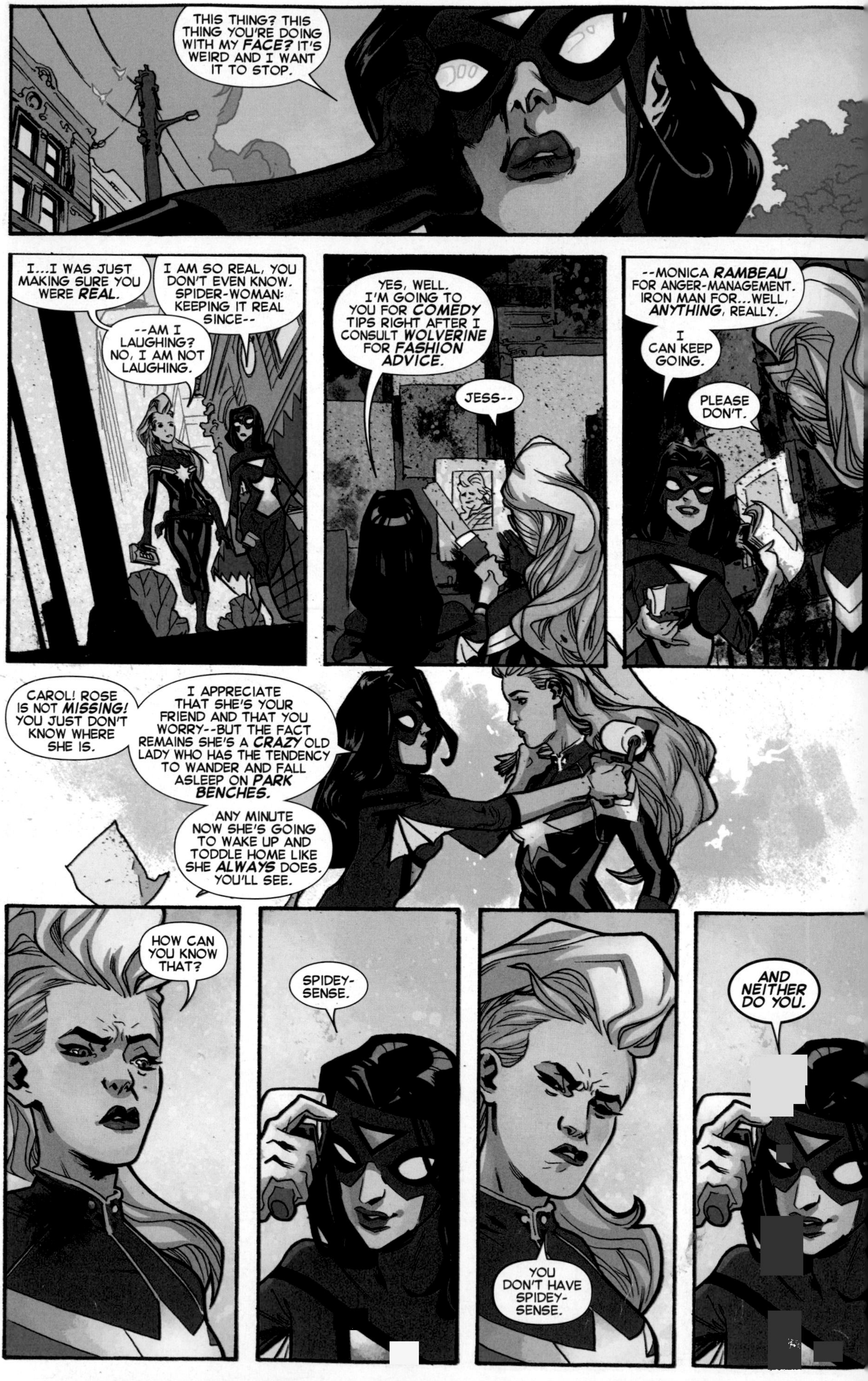
THIS THING? THIS THING YOU'RE DOING WITH MY FACE? IT'S WEIRD AND I WANT IT TO STOP.
I...I WAS JUST MAKING SURE YOU WERE REAL.
I AM SO REAL, YOU DON'T EVEN KNOW. SPIDER-WOMAN: KEEPING IT REAL SINCE--
--AM I LAUGHING? NO, I AM NOT LAUGHING.
YES, WELL. I'M GOING TO YOU FOR COMEDY TIPS RIGHT AFTER I CONSULT WOLVERINE FOR FASHION ADVICE.
JESS--
--MONICA RAMBEAU FOR ANGER-MANAGEMENT. IRON MAN FOR...WELL, ANYTHING, REALLY.
I CAN KEEP GOING.
PLEASE DON'T.
CAROL! ROSE IS NOT MISSING! YOU JUST DON'T KNOW WHERE SHE IS.
I APPRECIATE THAT SHE'S YOUR FRIEND AND THAT YOU WORRY--BUT THE FACT REMAINS SHE'S A CRAZY OLD LADY WHO HAS THE TENDENCY TO WANDER AND FALL ASLEEP ON PARK BENCHES.
ANY MINUTE NOW SHE'S GOING TO WAKE UP AND TODDLE HOME LIKE SHE ALWAYS DOES. YOU'LL SEE.
HOW CAN YOU KNOW THAT?
SPIDEY-SENSE.
YOU DON'T HAVE SPIDEY-SENSE.
AND NEITHER DO YOU.

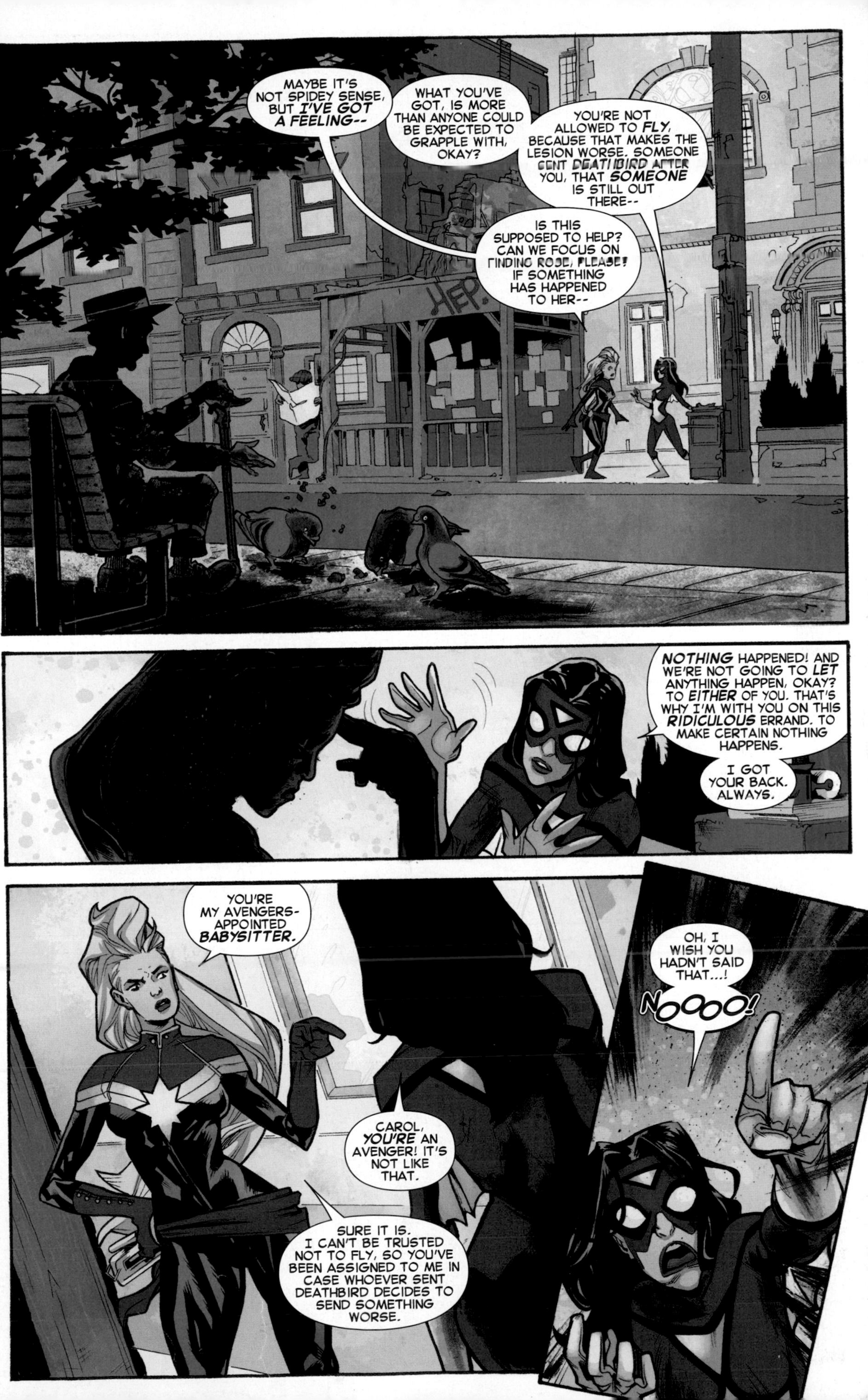
MAYBE IT'S NOT SPIDEY SENSE, BUT I'VE GOT A FEELING--
WHAT YOU'VE GOT, IS MORE THAN ANYONE COULD BE EXPECTED TO GRAPPLE WITH, OKAY?
YOU'RE NOT ALLOWED TO FLY, BECAUSE THAT MAKES THE LESION WORSE. SOMEONE SENT DEATHBIRD AFTER YOU, THAT SOMEONE IS STILL OUT THERE--
IS THIS SUPPOSED TO HELP? CAN WE FOCUS ON FINDING ROSE, PLEASE! IF SOMETHING HAS HAPPENED TO HER--
HEP.
NOTHING HAPPENED! AND WE'RE NOT GOING TO LET ANYTHING HAPPEN, OKAY? TO EITHER OF YOU. THAT'S WHY I'M WITH YOU ON THIS RIDICULOUS ERRAND. TO MAKE CERTAIN NOTHING HAPPENS.
I GOT YOUR BACK. ALWAYS.
YOU'RE MY AVENGERS-APPOINTED BABYSITTER.
CAROL, YOU'RE AN AVENGER! IT'S NOT LIKE THAT.
SURE IT IS. I CAN'T BE TRUSTED NOT TO FLY, SO YOU'VE BEEN ASSIGNED TO ME IN CASE WHOEVER SENT DEATHBIRD DECIDES TO SEND SOMETHING WORSE.
OH, I WISH YOU HADN'T SAID THAT...!
NOOOO!

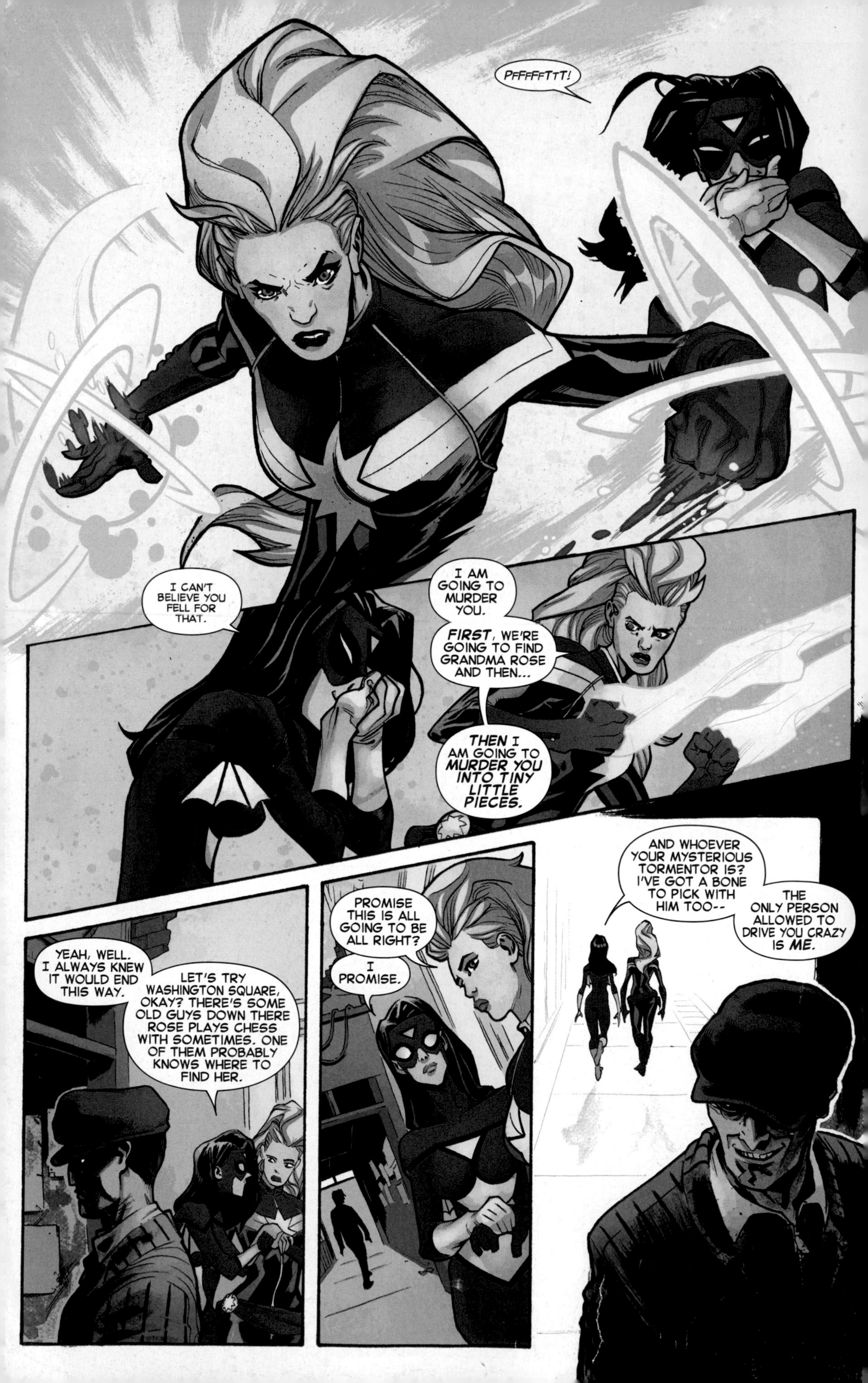
PFFFFFTTT!
I CAN'T BELIEVE YOU FELL FOR THAT.
I AM GOING TO MURDER YOU.
FIRST, WE'RE GOING TO FIND GRANDMA ROSE AND THEN...
THEN I AM GOING TO MURDER YOU INTO TINY LITTLE PIECES.
YEAH, WELL. I ALWAYS KNEW IT WOULD END THIS WAY.
LET'S TRY WASHINGTON SQUARE, OKAY? THERE'S SOME OLD GUYS DOWN THERE ROSE PLAYS CHESS WITH SOMETIMES. ONE OF THEM PROBABLY KNOWS WHERE TO FIND HER.
PROMISE THIS IS ALL GOING TO BE ALL RIGHT?
I PROMISE.
AND WHOEVER YOUR MYSTERIOUS TORMENTOR IS? I'VE GOT A BONE TO PICK WITH HIM TOO--
THE ONLY PERSON ALLOWED TO DRIVE YOU CRAZY IS ME.

When former U.S. Air Force pilot, Carol Danvers was caught in the explosion of an alien device called the Psyche-Magnitron, she was transformed into one of the world's most powerful super beings. She now uses her abilities to protect her planet and fight for justice as an Avenger. She is Earth's Mightiest Hero...she is...

CAPTAIN MARVEL

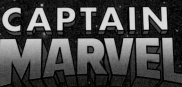

And there came a day, a day unlike any other, when Earth's mightiest heroes found themselves united against a common threat! On that day, the Avengers were born, to fight the foes no single super hero could withstand!

AVENGERS ASSEMBLE

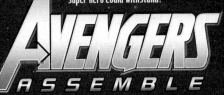

THE HARDEST FOE TO BEAT...

IS THE ONE INSIDE HER HEAD.

THE ENEMY WITHIN

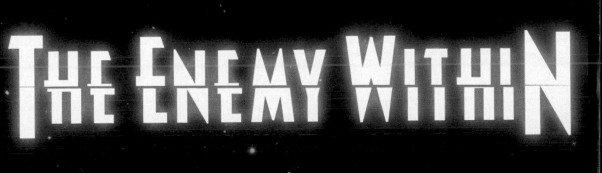

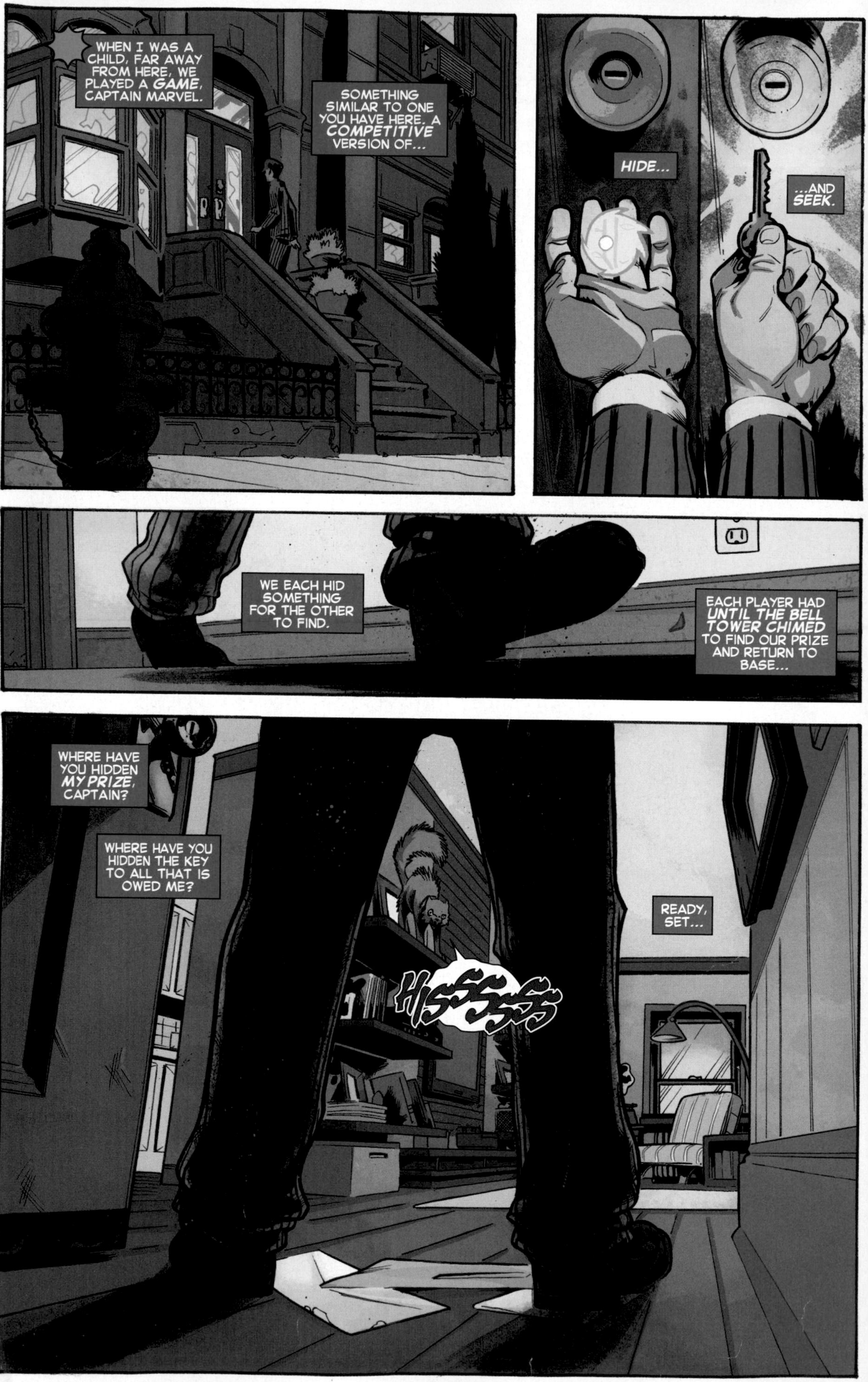
WHEN I WAS A CHILD, FAR AWAY FROM HERE, WE PLAYED A GAME, CAPTAIN MARVEL.
SOMETHING SIMILAR TO ONE YOU HAVE HERE. A COMPETITIVE VERSION OF...
HIDE...
...AND SEEK.
WE EACH HID SOMETHING FOR THE OTHER TO FIND.
EACH PLAYER HAD UNTIL THE BELL TOWER CHIMED TO FIND OUR PRIZE AND RETURN TO BASE...
WHERE HAVE YOU HIDDEN MY PRIZE, CAPTAIN?
WHERE HAVE YOU HIDDEN THE KEY TO ALL THAT IS OWED ME?
READY, SET...
HISSSSSS

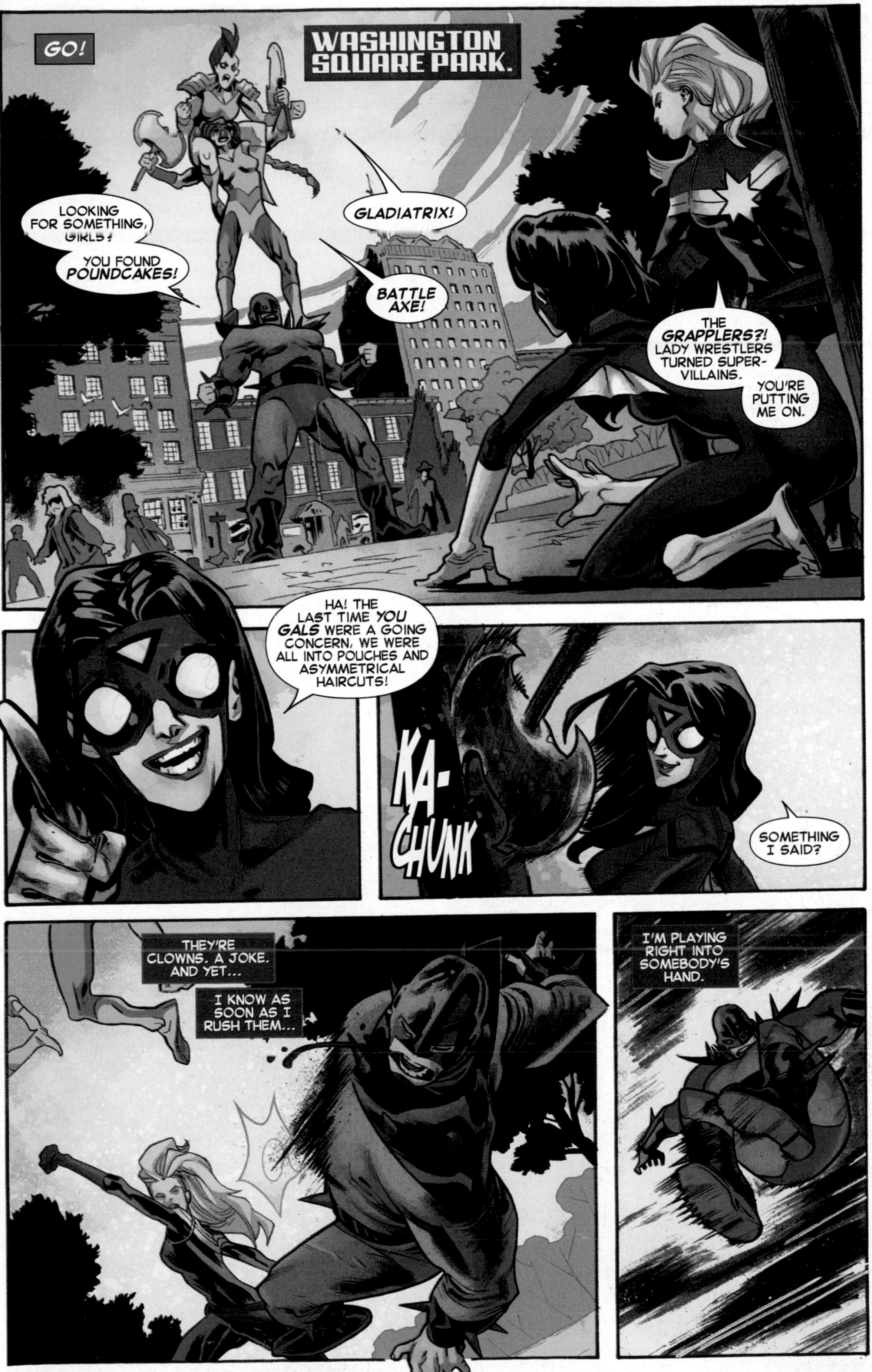
GO!
WASHINGTON SQUARE PARK.
LOOKING FOR SOMETHING, GIRLS?
YOU FOUND POUNDCAKES!
GLADIATRIX!
BATTLE AXE!
THE GRAPPLERS?! LADY WRESTLERS TURNED SUPER-VILLAINS.
YOU'RE PUTTING ME ON.
HA! THE LAST TIME YOU GALS WERE A GOING CONCERN, WE WERE ALL INTO POUCHES AND ASYMMETRICAL HAIRCUTS!
KA-CHUNK
SOMETHING I SAID?
THEY'RE CLOWNS. A JOKE. AND YET...
I KNOW AS SOON AS I RUSH THEM...
I'M PLAYING RIGHT INTO SOMEBODY'S HAND.

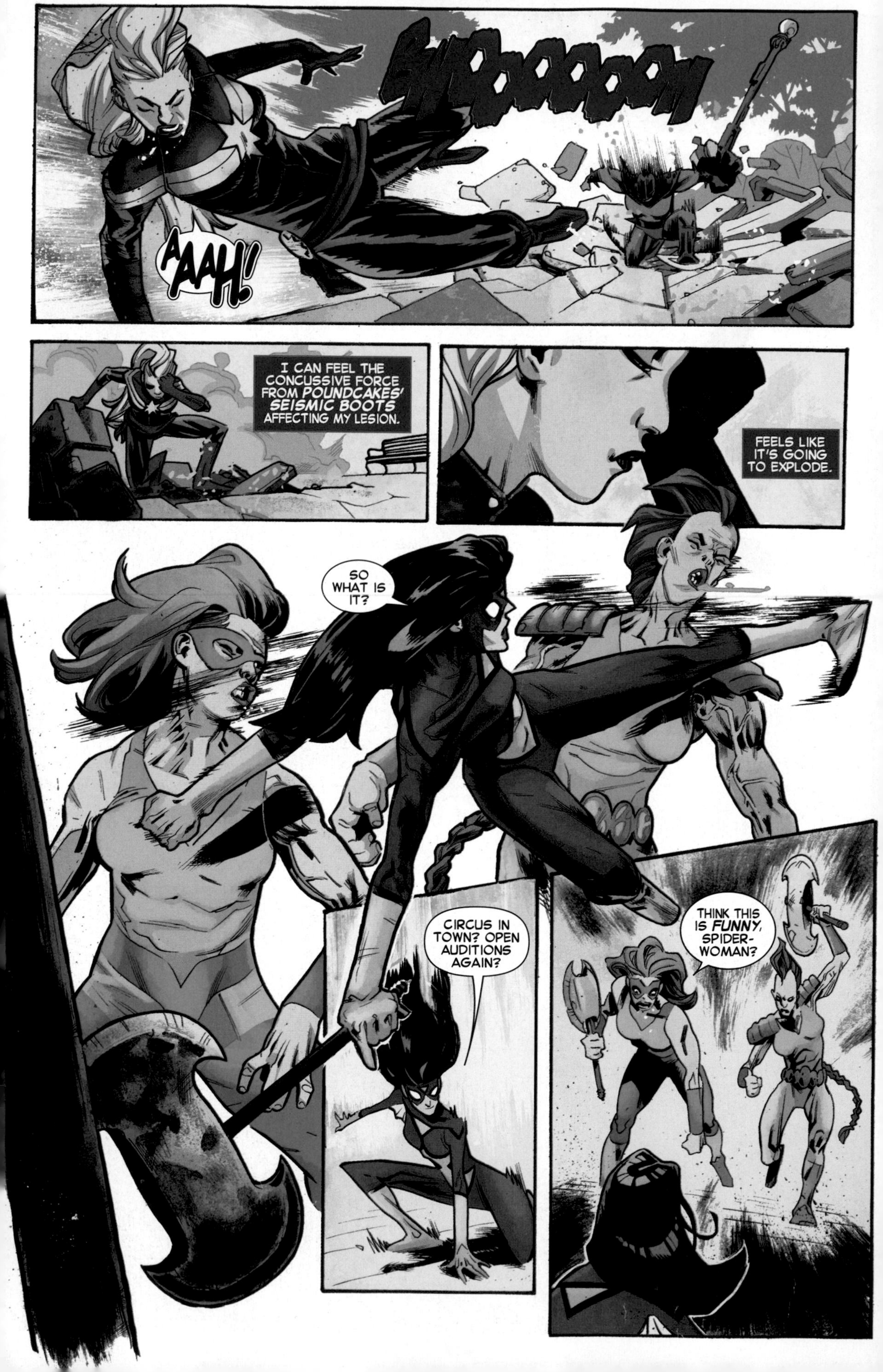
BHOOOOOOM
AAAH!
I CAN FEEL THE CONCUSSIVE FORCE FROM POUNDCAKES' SEISMIC BOOTS AFFECTING MY LESION.
FEELS LIKE IT'S GOING TO EXPLODE.
SO WHAT IS IT?
CIRCUS IN TOWN? OPEN AUDITIONS AGAIN?
THINK THIS IS FUNNY, SPIDER-WOMAN?

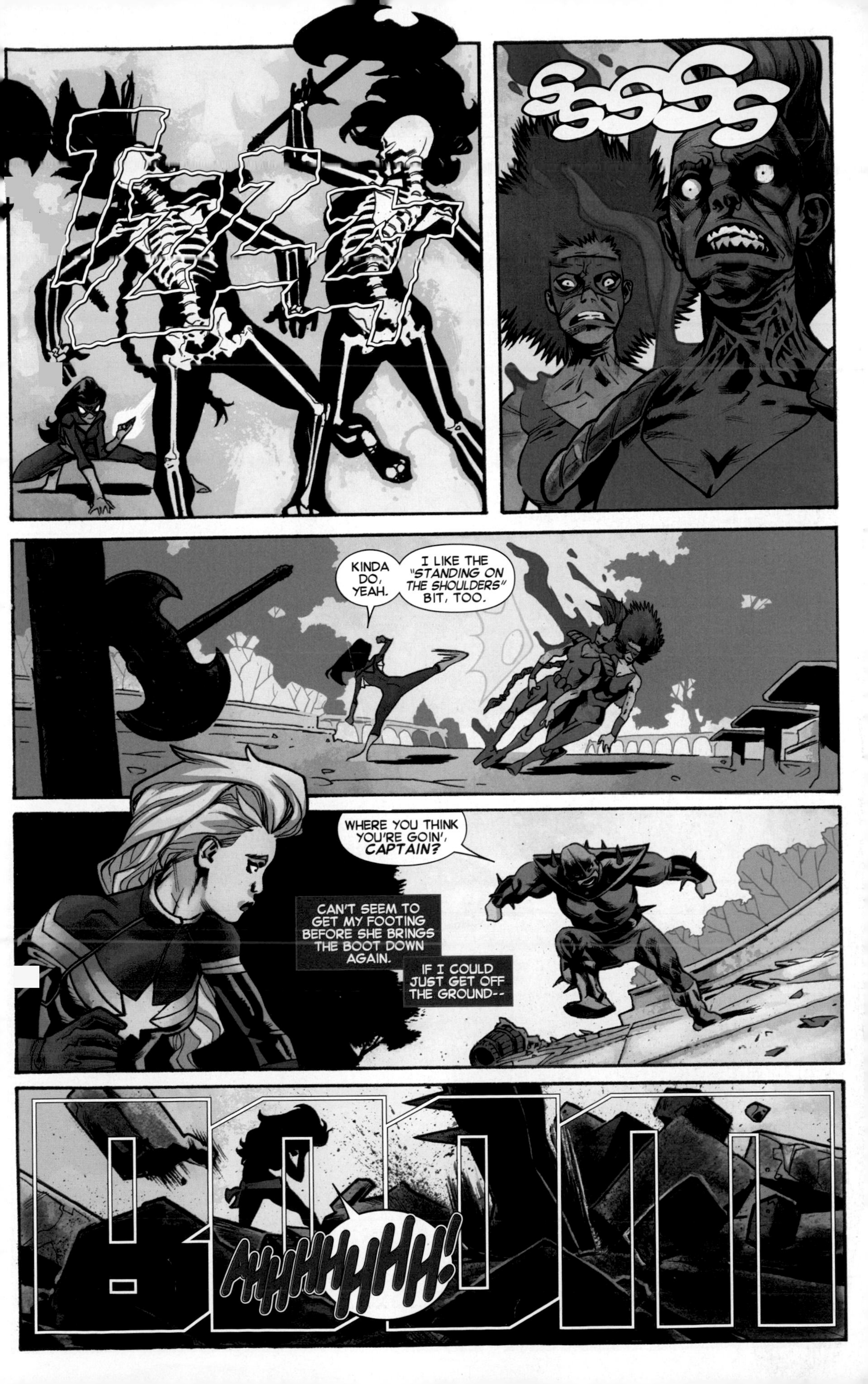

ZZZT
SSSSS
KINDA DO, YEAH.
I LIKE THE "STANDING ON THE SHOULDERS" BIT, TOO.
WHERE YOU THINK YOU'RE GOIN', CAPTAIN?
CAN'T SEEM TO GET MY FOOTING BEFORE SHE BRINGS THE BOOT DOWN AGAIN.
IF I COULD JUST GET OFF THE GROUND--
AHHHHHHHH!

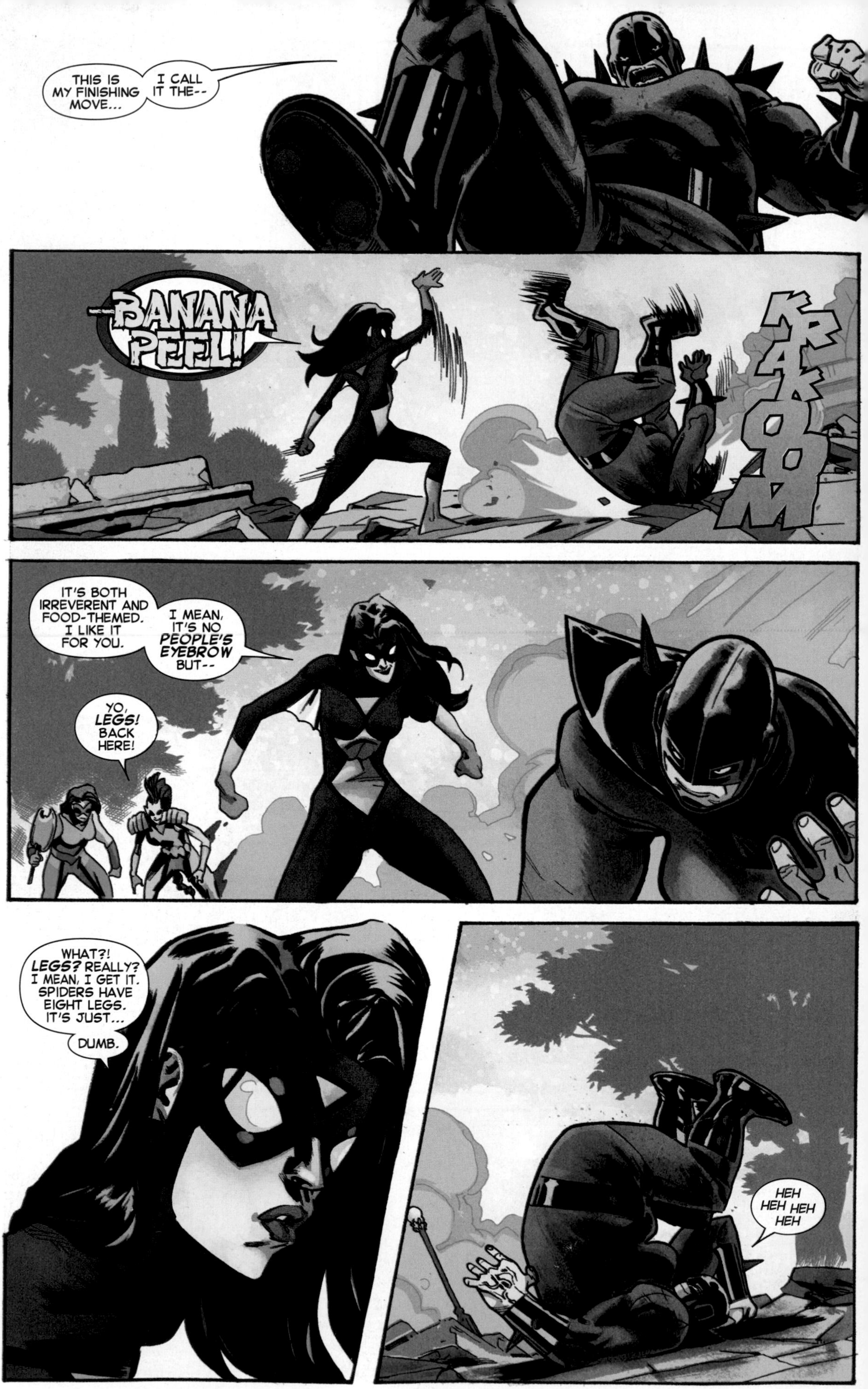
THIS IS MY FINISHING MOVE...
I CALL IT THE--
BANANA PEEL!
KRAKOOM
IT'S BOTH IRREVERENT AND FOOD-THEMED. I LIKE IT FOR YOU.
I MEAN, IT'S NO PEOPLE'S EYEBROW BUT--
YO, LEGS! BACK HERE!
WHAT?! LEGS? REALLY? I MEAN, I GET IT. SPIDERS HAVE EIGHT LEGS. IT'S JUST...
DUMB.
HEH HEH HEH HEH

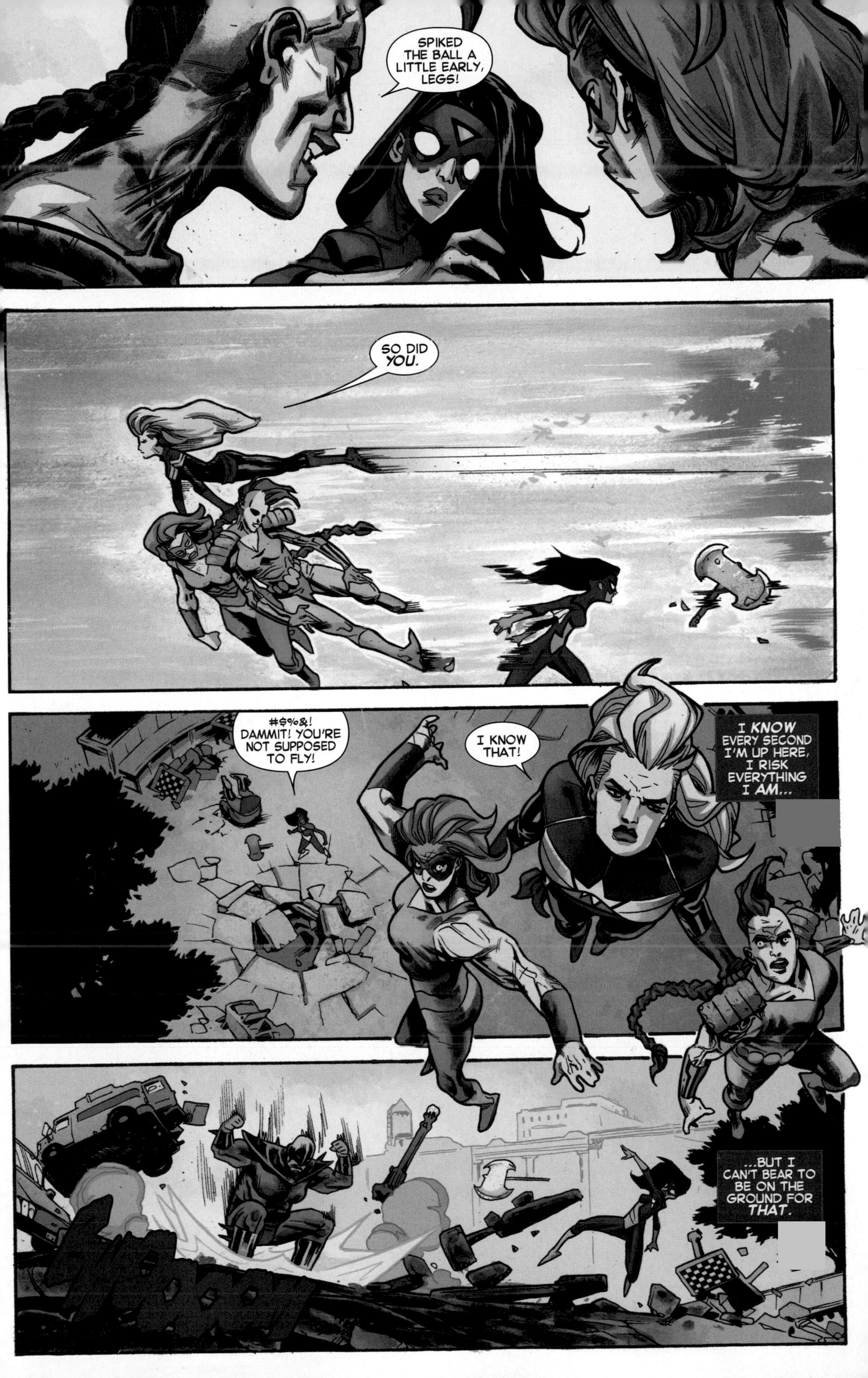
SPIKED THE BALL A LITTLE EARLY, LEGS!
SO DID YOU.
#$%&! DAMMIT! YOU'RE NOT SUPPOSED TO FLY!
I KNOW THAT!
I KNOW EVERY SECOND I'M UP HERE, I RISK EVERYTHING I AM...
...BUT I CAN'T BEAR TO BE ON THE GROUND FOR THAT.

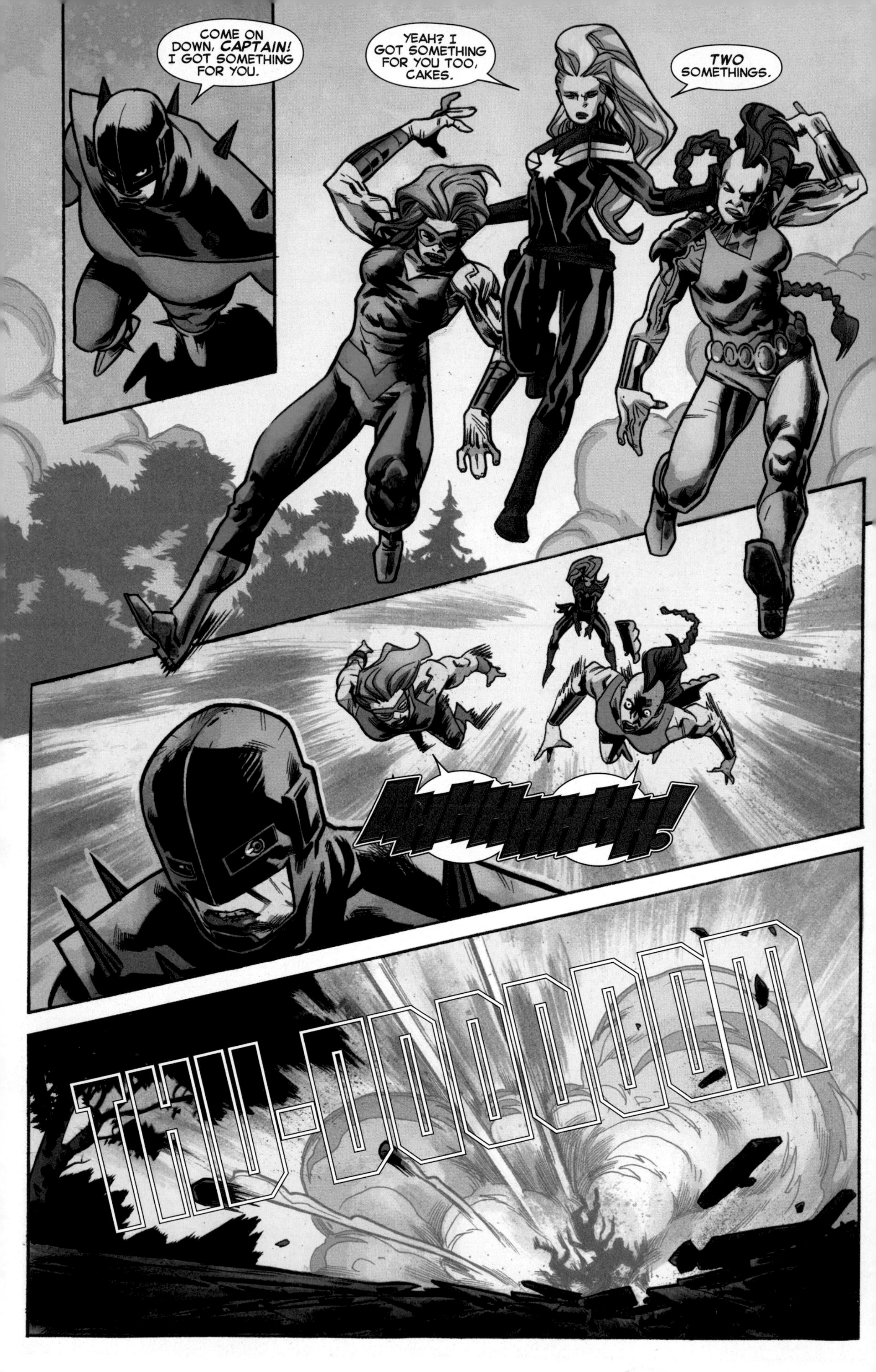
COME ON DOWN, CAPTAIN! I GOT SOMETHING FOR YOU.
YEAH? I GOT SOMETHING FOR YOU TOO, CAKES.
TWO SOMETHINGS.
AHHHHHHHH!
THU-DOOOOOM

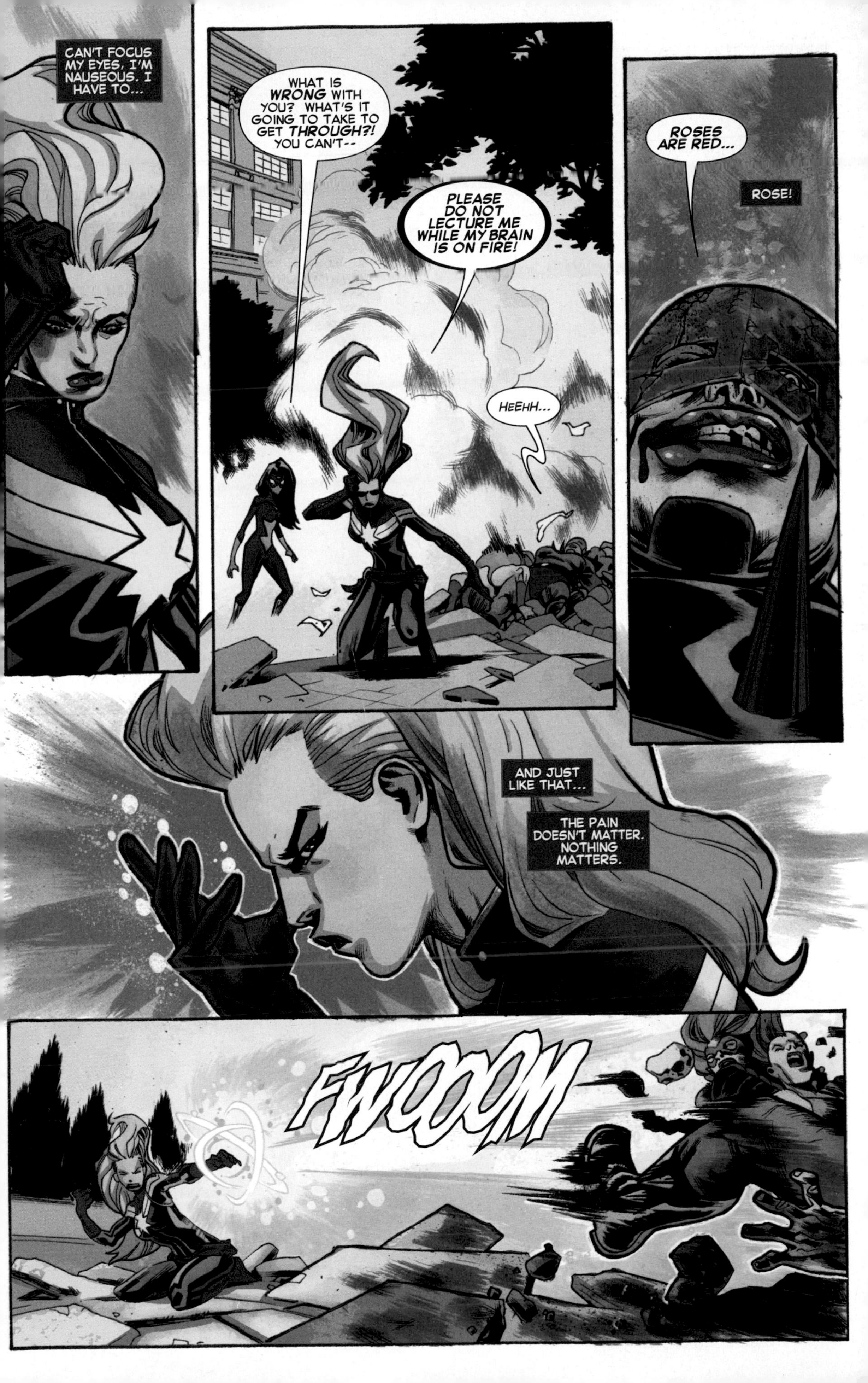
CAN'T FOCUS MY EYES, I'M NAUSEOUS. I HAVE TO...
WHAT IS WRONG WITH YOU? WHAT'S IT GOING TO TAKE TO GET THROUGH?! YOU CAN'T--
PLEASE DO NOT LECTURE ME WHILE MY BRAIN IS ON FIRE!
HEEHH...
ROSES ARE RED...
ROSE!
AND JUST LIKE THAT...
THE PAIN DOESN'T MATTER. NOTHING MATTERS.
FWOOOM

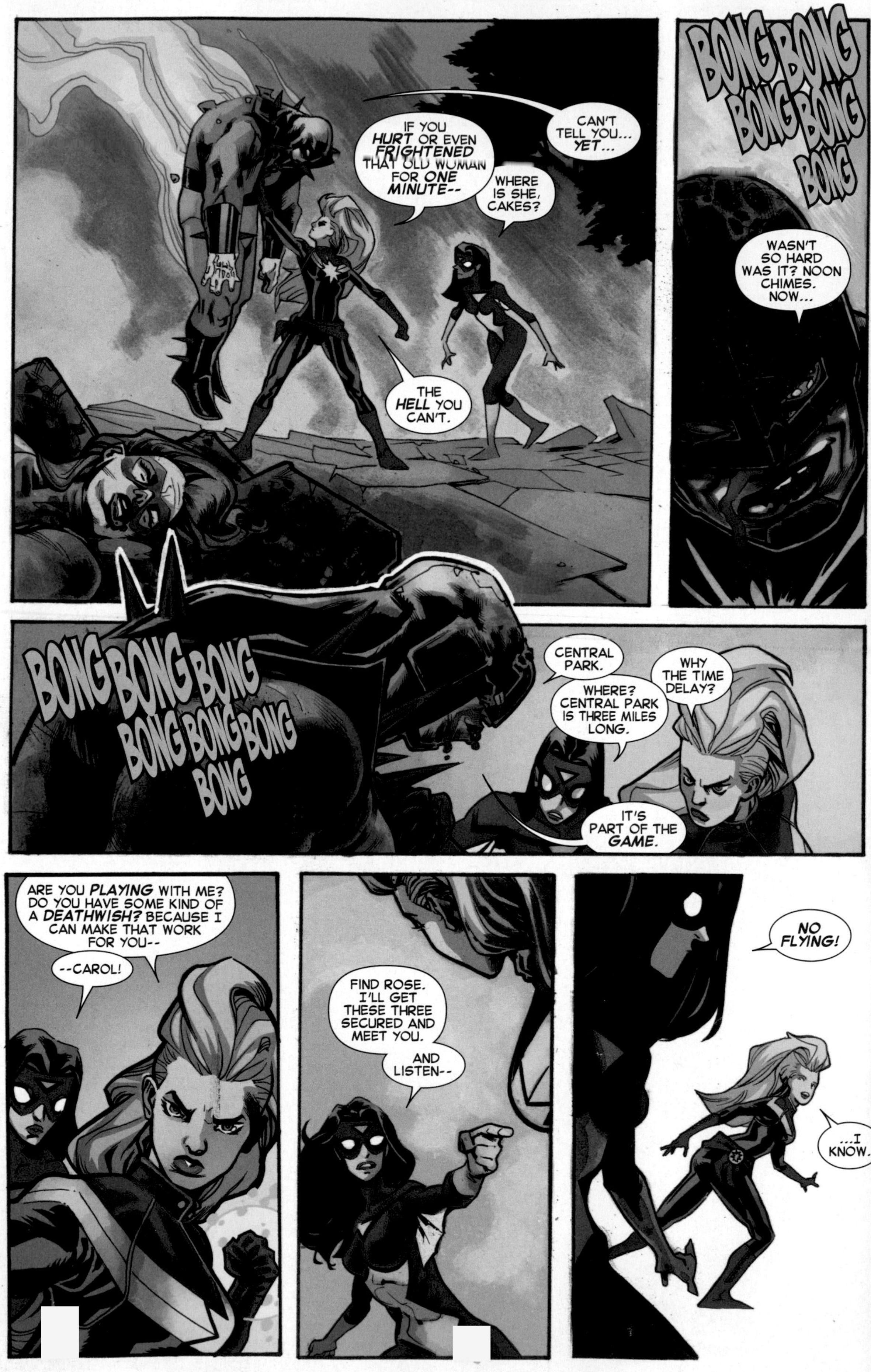
IF YOU HURT OR EVEN FRIGHTENED THAT OLD WOMAN FOR ONE MINUTE--
CAN'T TELL YOU... YET...
WHERE IS SHE, CAKES?
THE HELL YOU CAN'T.
BONG BONG BONG BONG BONG
WASN'T SO HARD WAS IT? NOON CHIMES. NOW...
BONG BONG BONG BONG BONG BONG BONG
CENTRAL PARK.
WHERE? CENTRAL PARK IS THREE MILES LONG.
WHY THE TIME DELAY?
IT'S PART OF THE GAME.
ARE YOU PLAYING WITH ME? DO YOU HAVE SOME KIND OF A DEATHWISH? BECAUSE I CAN MAKE THAT WORK FOR YOU--
--CAROL!
FIND ROSE. I'LL GET THESE THREE SECURED AND MEET YOU.
AND LISTEN--
NO FLYING!
...I KNOW.

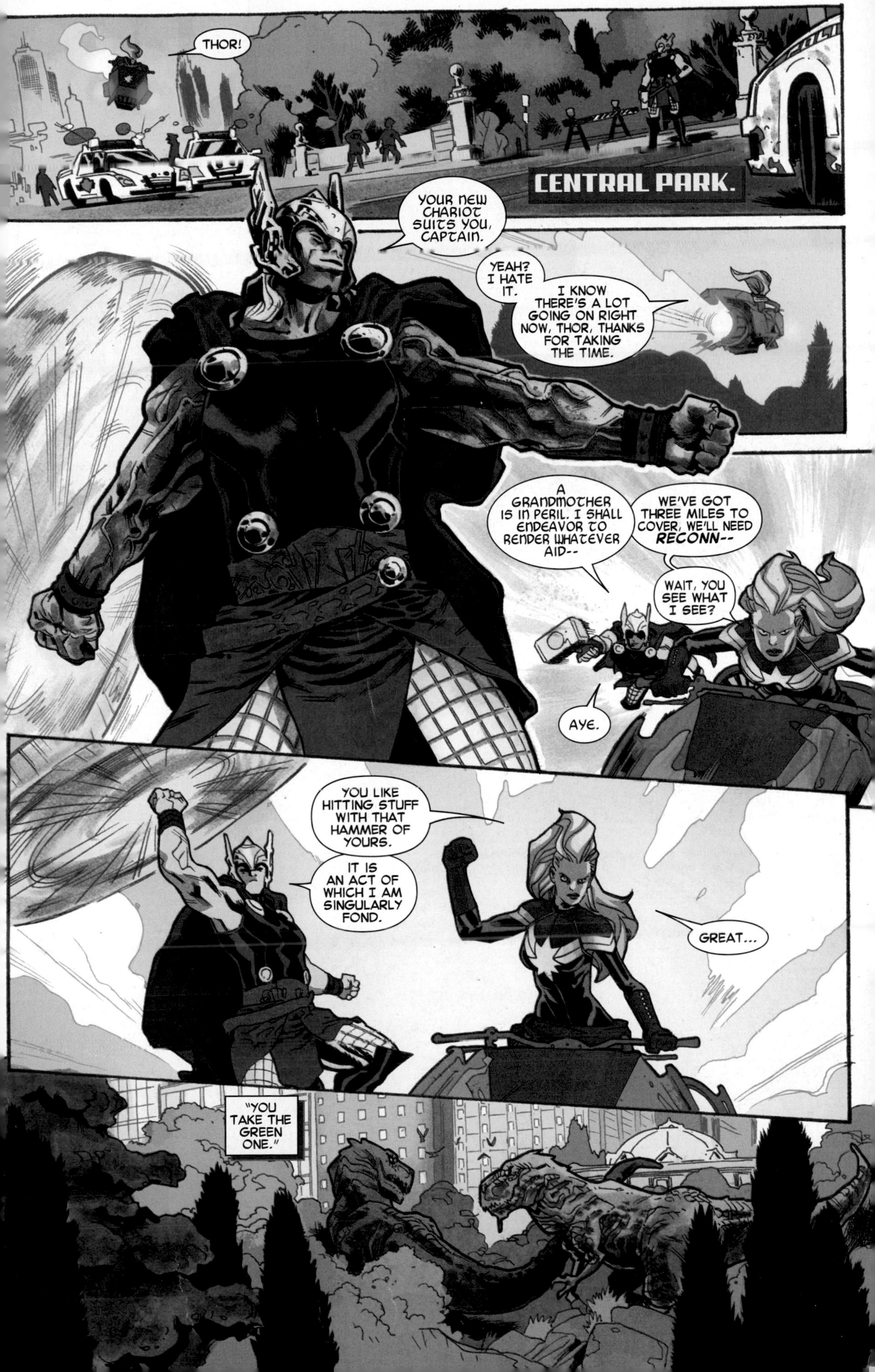
THOR!
CENTRAL PARK.
YOUR NEW CHARIOT SUITS YOU, CAPTAIN.
YEAH? I HATE IT.
I KNOW THERE'S A LOT GOING ON RIGHT NOW, THOR, THANKS FOR TAKING THE TIME.
A GRANDMOTHER IS IN PERIL. I SHALL ENDEAVOR TO RENDER WHATEVER AID--
WE'VE GOT THREE MILES TO COVER, WE'LL NEED RECONN--
WAIT, YOU SEE WHAT I SEE?
AYE.
YOU LIKE HITTING STUFF WITH THAT HAMMER OF YOURS.
IT IS AN ACT OF WHICH I AM SINGULARLY FOND.
GREAT...
"YOU TAKE THE GREEN ONE."

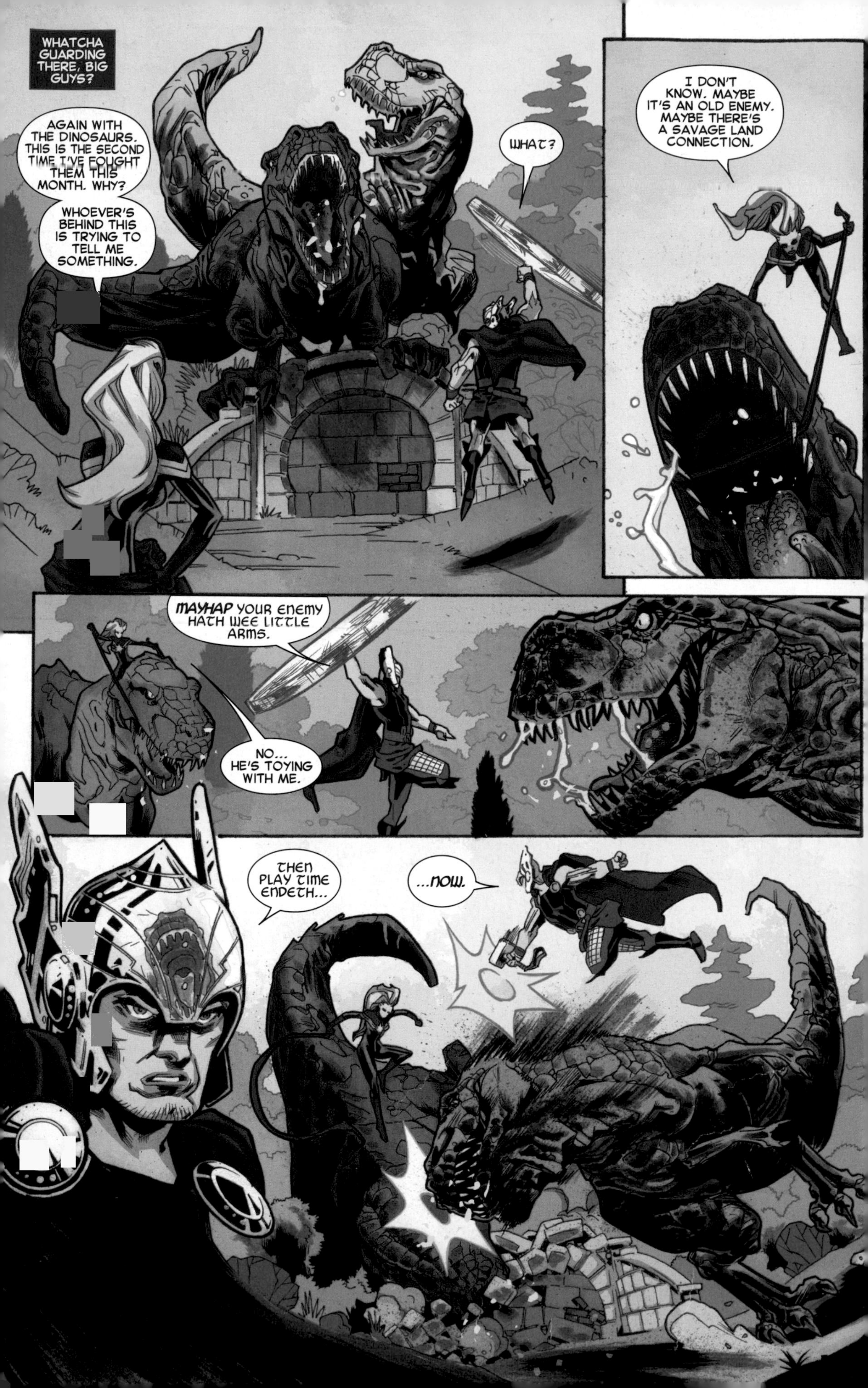
WHATCHA GUARDING THERE, BIG GUYS?
AGAIN WITH THE DINOSAURS. THIS IS THE SECOND TIME I'VE FOUGHT THEM THIS MONTH. WHY?
WHOEVER'S BEHIND THIS IS TRYING TO TELL ME SOMETHING.
WHAT?
I DON'T KNOW. MAYBE IT'S AN OLD ENEMY. MAYBE THERE'S A SAVAGE LAND CONNECTION.
MAYHAP YOUR ENEMY HATH WEE LITTLE ARMS.
NO... HE'S TOYING WITH ME.
THEN PLAY TIME ENDETH...
...NOW.

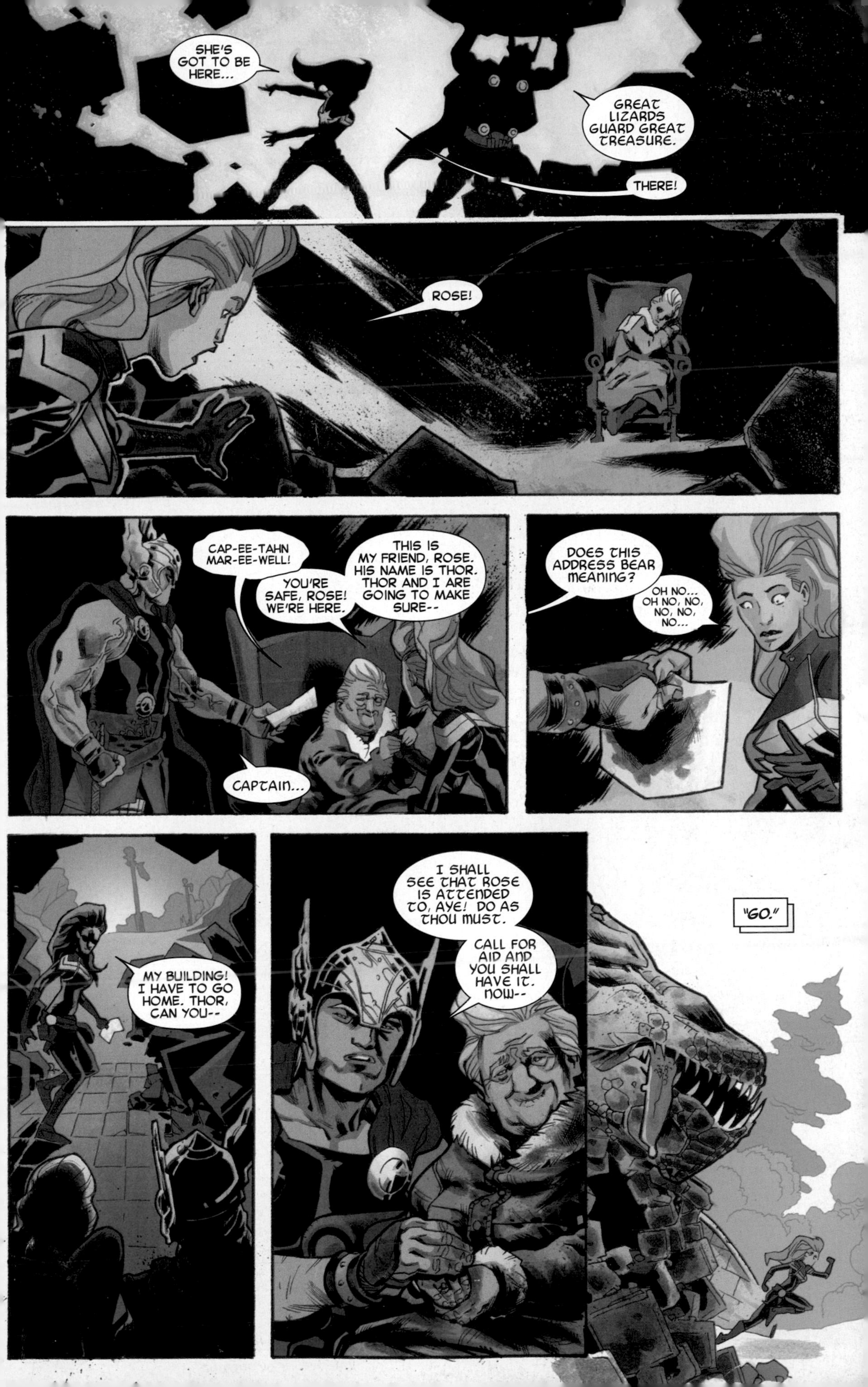
SHE'S GOT TO BE HERE...
GREAT LIZARDS GUARD GREAT TREASURE.
THERE!
ROSE!
CAP-EE-TAHN MAR-EE-WELL!
YOU'RE SAFE, ROSE! WE'RE HERE.
THIS IS MY FRIEND, ROSE. HIS NAME IS THOR. THOR AND I ARE GOING TO MAKE SURE--
CAPTAIN...
DOES THIS ADDRESS BEAR MEANING?
OH NO... OH NO, NO, NO, NO, NO...
MY BUILDING! I HAVE TO GO HOME. THOR, CAN YOU--
I SHALL SEE THAT ROSE IS ATTENDED TO, AYE! DO AS THOU MUST.
CALL FOR AID AND YOU SHALL HAVE IT. NOW--
"GO."

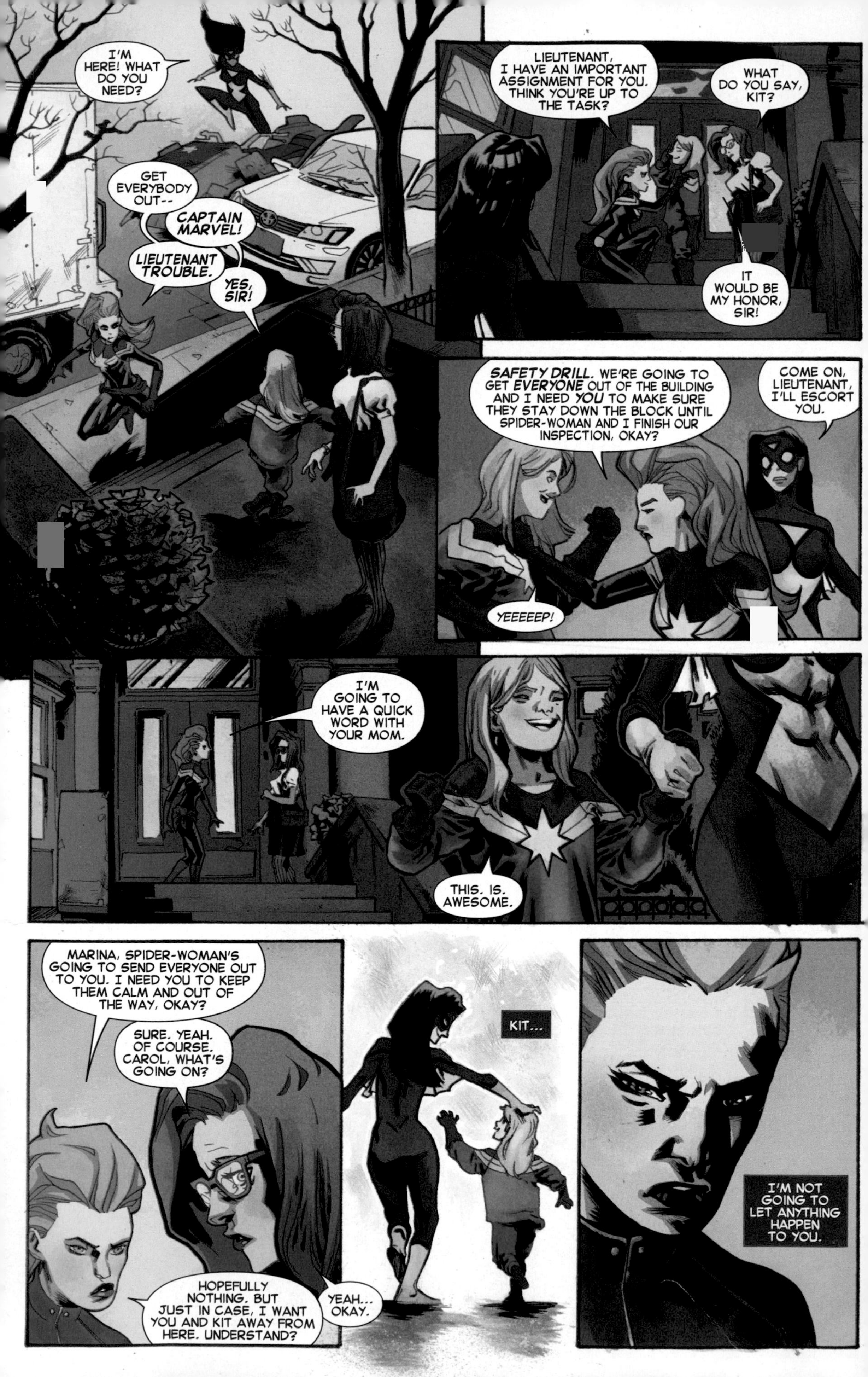
I'M HERE! WHAT DO YOU NEED?
GET EVERYBODY OUT--
CAPTAIN MARVEL!
LIEUTENANT TROUBLE.
YES, SIR!
LIEUTENANT, I HAVE AN IMPORTANT ASSIGNMENT FOR YOU. THINK YOU'RE UP TO THE TASK?
WHAT DO YOU SAY, KIT?
IT WOULD BE MY HONOR, SIR!
SAFETY DRILL. WE'RE GOING TO GET EVERYONE OUT OF THE BUILDING AND I NEED YOU TO MAKE SURE THEY STAY DOWN THE BLOCK UNTIL SPIDER-WOMAN AND I FINISH OUR INSPECTION, OKAY?
COME ON, LIEUTENANT, I'LL ESCORT YOU.
YEEEEEP!
I'M GOING TO HAVE A QUICK WORD WITH YOUR MOM.
THIS. IS. AWESOME.
MARINA, SPIDER-WOMAN'S GOING TO SEND EVERYONE OUT TO YOU. I NEED YOU TO KEEP THEM CALM AND OUT OF THE WAY, OKAY?
SURE. YEAH. OF COURSE. CAROL, WHAT'S GOING ON?
HOPEFULLY NOTHING. BUT JUST IN CASE, I WANT YOU AND KIT AWAY FROM HERE. UNDERSTAND?
YEAH... OKAY.
KIT...
I'M NOT GOING TO LET ANYTHING HAPPEN TO YOU.

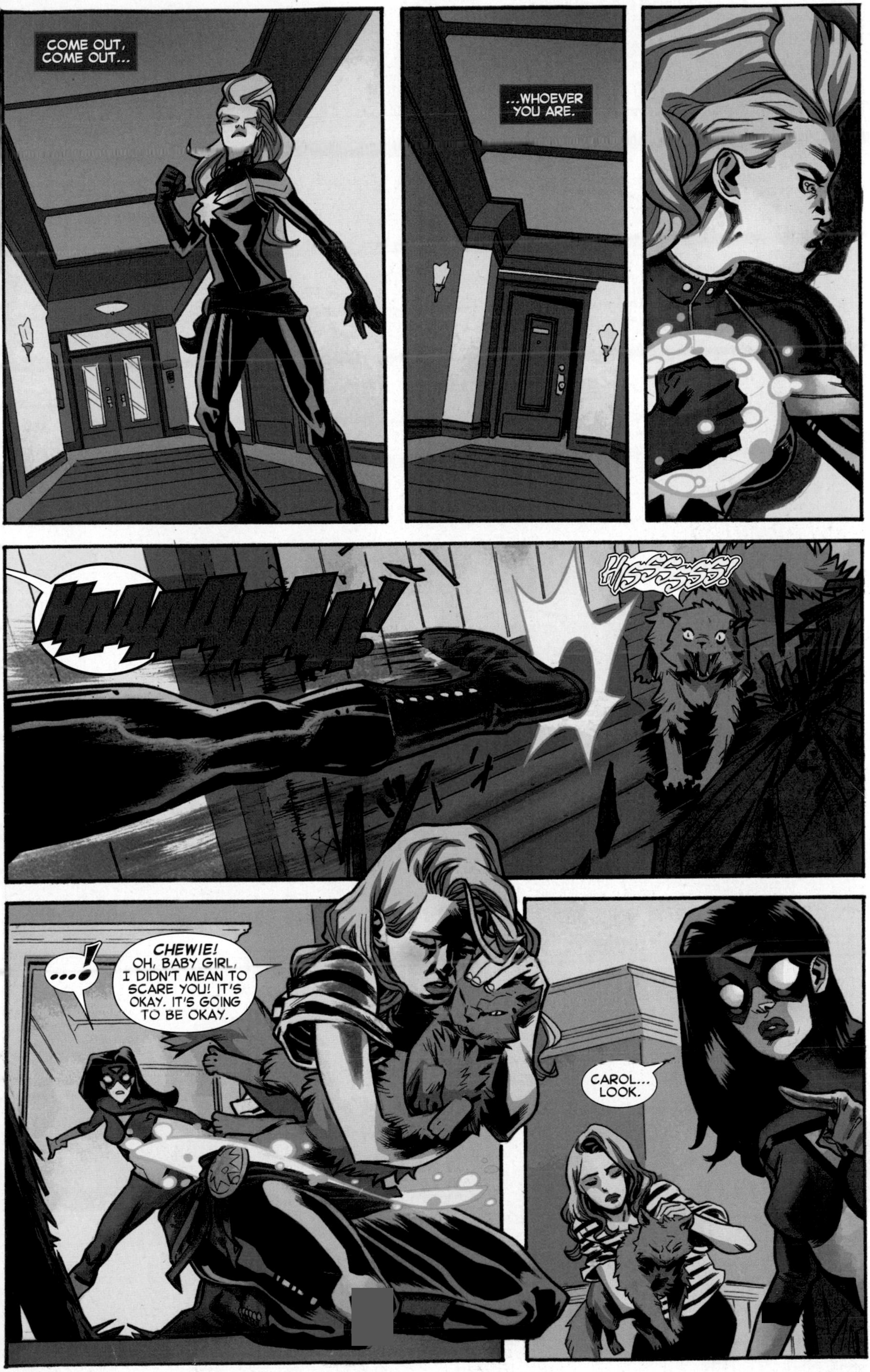
COME OUT, COME OUT...
...WHOEVER YOU ARE.
HISSSSSS!
...!
CHEWIE! OH, BABY GIRL, I DIDN'T MEAN TO SCARE YOU! IT'S OKAY. IT'S GOING TO BE OKAY.
CAROL... LOOK.

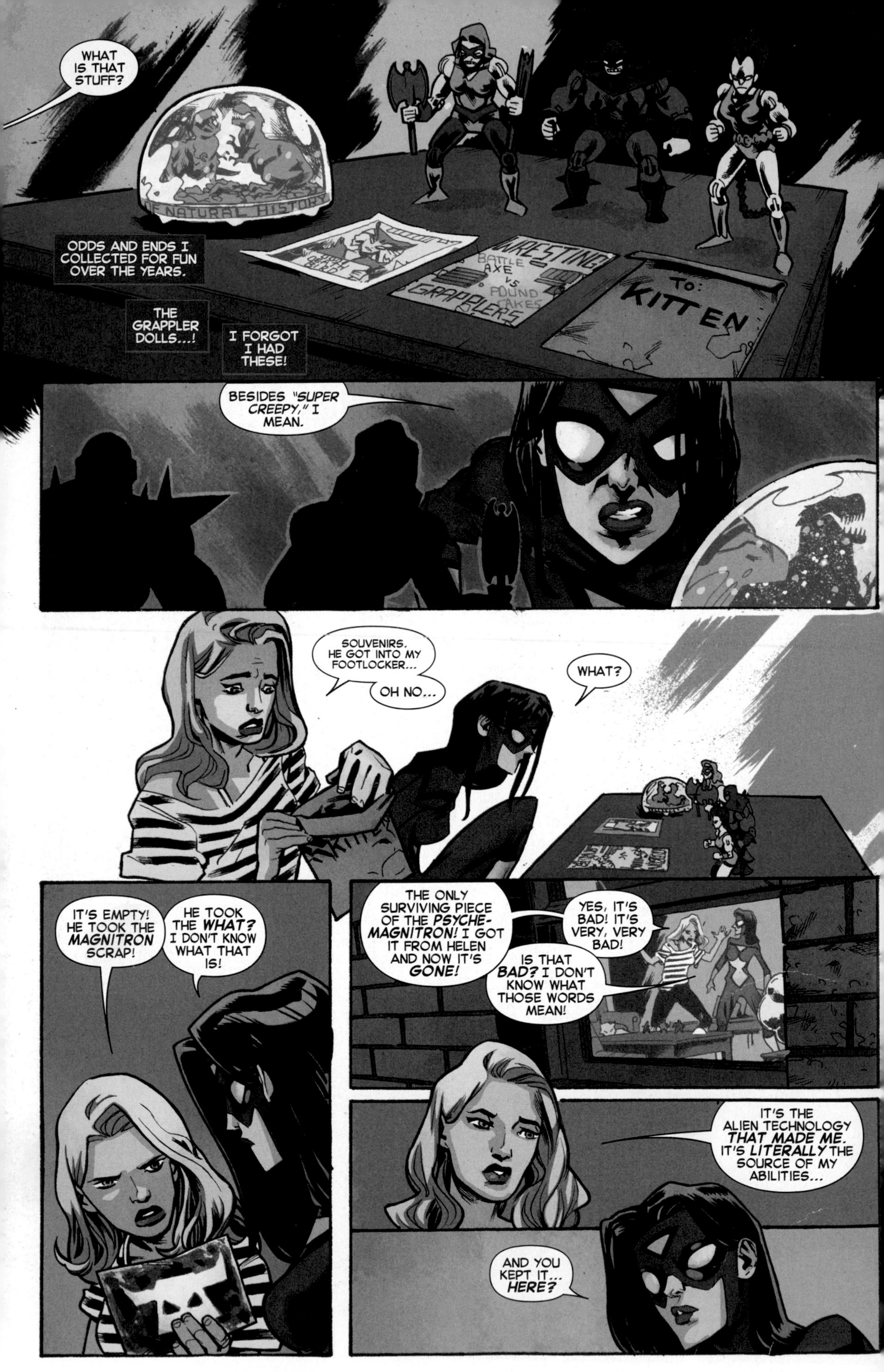
WHAT IS THAT STUFF?
ODDS AND ENDS I COLLECTED FOR FUN OVER THE YEARS.
THE GRAPPLER DOLLS...!
I FORGOT I HAD THESE!
WRESTING
BATTLE AXE VS POUND CAKES
GRAPPLERS
TO: KITTEN
BESIDES "SUPER CREEPY," I MEAN.
SOUVENIRS. HE GOT INTO MY FOOTLOCKER...
OH NO...
WHAT?
IT'S EMPTY! HE TOOK THE MAGNITRON SCRAP!
HE TOOK THE WHAT? I DON'T KNOW WHAT THAT IS!
THE ONLY SURVIVING PIECE OF THE PSYCHE-MAGNITRON! I GOT IT FROM HELEN AND NOW IT'S GONE!
IS THAT BAD? I DON'T KNOW WHAT THOSE WORDS MEAN!
YES, IT'S BAD! IT'S VERY, VERY BAD!
IT'S THE ALIEN TECHNOLOGY THAT MADE ME. IT'S LITERALLY THE SOURCE OF MY ABILITIES...
AND YOU KEPT IT... HERE?

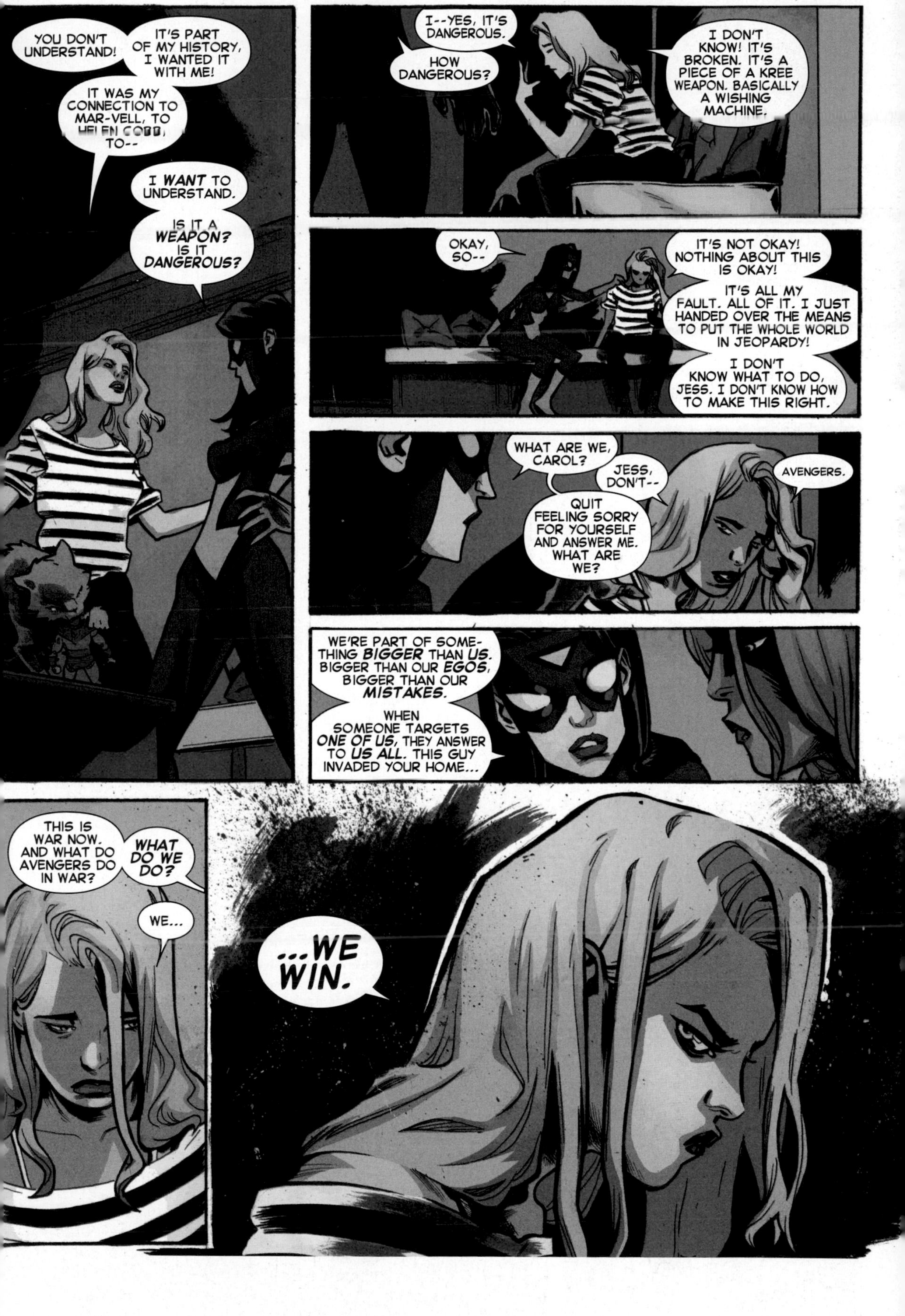

YOU DON'T UNDERSTAND!
IT'S PART OF MY HISTORY, I WANTED IT WITH ME!
IT WAS MY CONNECTION TO MAR-VELL, TO HELEN COBB, TO--
I WANT TO UNDERSTAND.
IS IT A WEAPON? IS IT DANGEROUS?
I--YES, IT'S DANGEROUS.
HOW DANGEROUS?
I DON'T KNOW! IT'S BROKEN. IT'S A PIECE OF A KREE WEAPON. BASICALLY A WISHING MACHINE.
OKAY, SO--
IT'S NOT OKAY! NOTHING ABOUT THIS IS OKAY!
IT'S ALL MY FAULT. ALL OF IT. I JUST HANDED OVER THE MEANS TO PUT THE WHOLE WORLD IN JEOPARDY!
I DON'T KNOW WHAT TO DO, JESS. I DON'T KNOW HOW TO MAKE THIS RIGHT.
WHAT ARE WE, CAROL?
JESS, DON'T--
QUIT FEELING SORRY FOR YOURSELF AND ANSWER ME. WHAT ARE WE?
AVENGERS.
WE'RE PART OF SOMETHING BIGGER THAN US. BIGGER THAN OUR EGOS, BIGGER THAN OUR MISTAKES.
WHEN SOMEONE TARGETS ONE OF US, THEY ANSWER TO US ALL. THIS GUY INVADED YOUR HOME...
THIS IS WAR NOW. AND WHAT DO AVENGERS DO IN WAR?
WHAT DO WE DO?
WE...
...WE WIN.

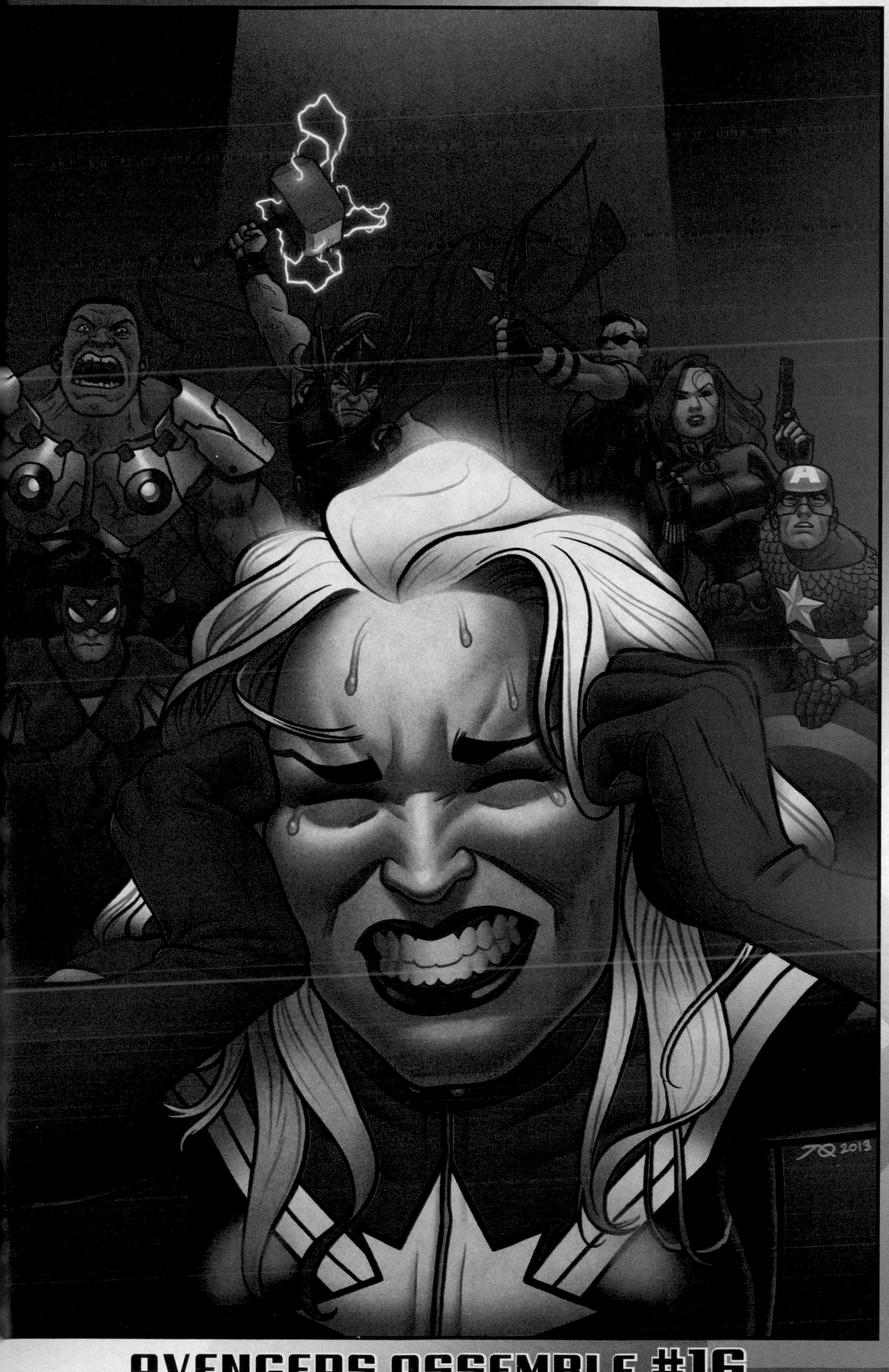
JQ 2013

AVENGERS ASSEMBLE #16

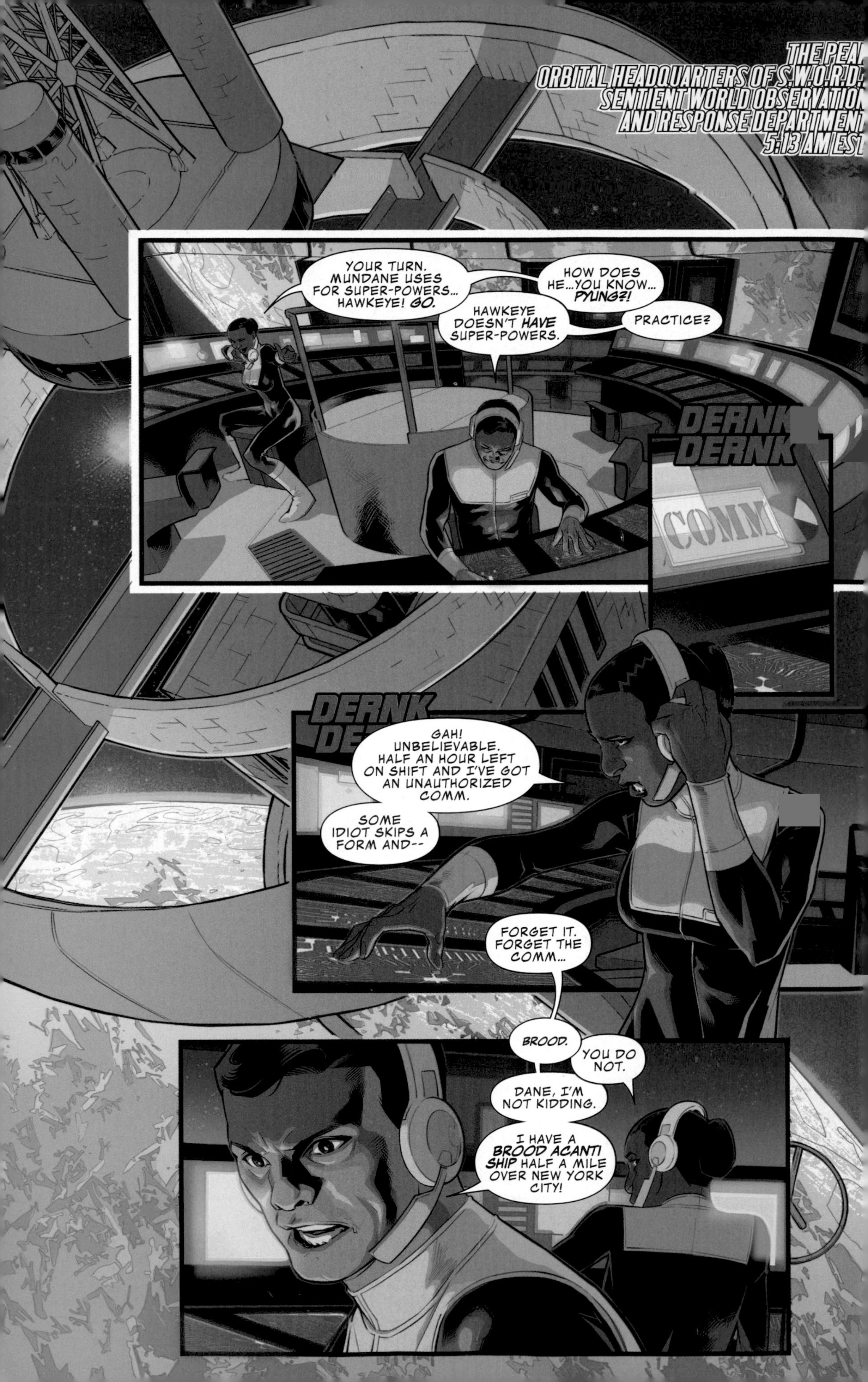

THE PEA
ORBITAL HEADQUARTERS OF S.W.O.R.D.:
SENTIENT WORLD OBSERVATIO
AND RESPONSE DEPARTMEN
5:13 AM ES
YOUR TURN. MUNDANE USES FOR SUPER-POWERS... HAWKEYE! GO.
HOW DOES HE...YOU KNOW... PYUNG?!
HAWKEYE DOESN'T HAVE SUPER-POWERS.
PRACTICE?
DERNK
DERNK
COMM
DERNK
DE
GAH! UNBELIEVABLE. HALF AN HOUR LEFT ON SHIFT AND I'VE GOT AN UNAUTHORIZED COMM.
SOME IDIOT SKIPS A FORM AND--
FORGET IT. FORGET THE COMM...
BROOD.
YOU DO NOT.
DANE, I'M NOT KIDDING.
I HAVE A BROOD ACANTI SHIP HALF A MILE OVER NEW YORK CITY!

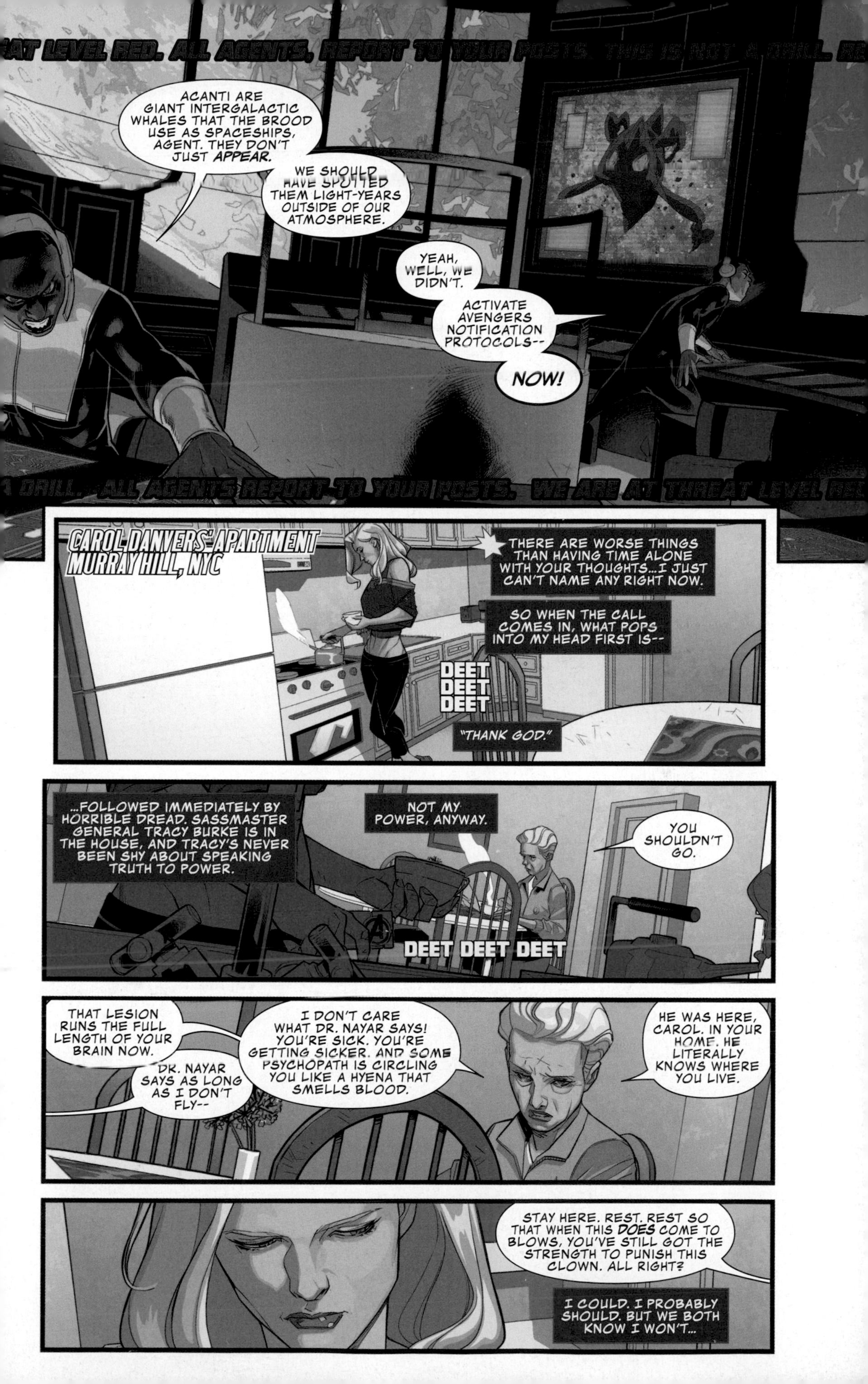
...AT LEVEL RED. ALL AGENTS, REPORT TO YOUR POSTS. THIS IS NOT A DRILL. RE...
ACANTI ARE GIANT INTERGALACTIC WHALES THAT THE BROOD USE AS SPACESHIPS, AGENT. THEY DON'T JUST APPEAR.
WE SHOULD HAVE SPOTTED THEM LIGHT-YEARS OUTSIDE OF OUR ATMOSPHERE.
YEAH, WELL, WE DIDN'T.
ACTIVATE AVENGERS NOTIFICATION PROTOCOLS--
NOW!
...A DRILL. ALL AGENTS REPORT TO YOUR POSTS. WE ARE AT THREAT LEVEL RED...
CAROL DANVERS' APARTMENT MURRAY HILL, NYC
THERE ARE WORSE THINGS THAN HAVING TIME ALONE WITH YOUR THOUGHTS...I JUST CAN'T NAME ANY RIGHT NOW.
SO WHEN THE CALL COMES IN, WHAT POPS INTO MY HEAD FIRST IS--
DEET DEET DEET
"THANK GOD."
...FOLLOWED IMMEDIATELY BY HORRIBLE DREAD. SASSMASTER GENERAL TRACY BURKE IS IN THE HOUSE, AND TRACY'S NEVER BEEN SHY ABOUT SPEAKING TRUTH TO POWER.
NOT MY POWER, ANYWAY.
YOU SHOULDN'T GO.
DEET DEET DEET
THAT LESION RUNS THE FULL LENGTH OF YOUR BRAIN NOW.
DR. NAYAR SAYS AS LONG AS I DON'T FLY--
I DON'T CARE WHAT DR. NAYAR SAYS! YOU'RE SICK. YOU'RE GETTING SICKER. AND SOME PSYCHOPATH IS CIRCLING YOU LIKE A HYENA THAT SMELLS BLOOD.
HE WAS HERE, CAROL. IN YOUR HOME. HE LITERALLY KNOWS WHERE YOU LIVE.
STAY HERE. REST. REST SO THAT WHEN THIS DOES COME TO BLOWS, YOU'VE STILL GOT THE STRENGTH TO PUNISH THIS CLOWN. ALL RIGHT?
I COULD. I PROBABLY SHOULD. BUT WE BOTH KNOW I WON'T...

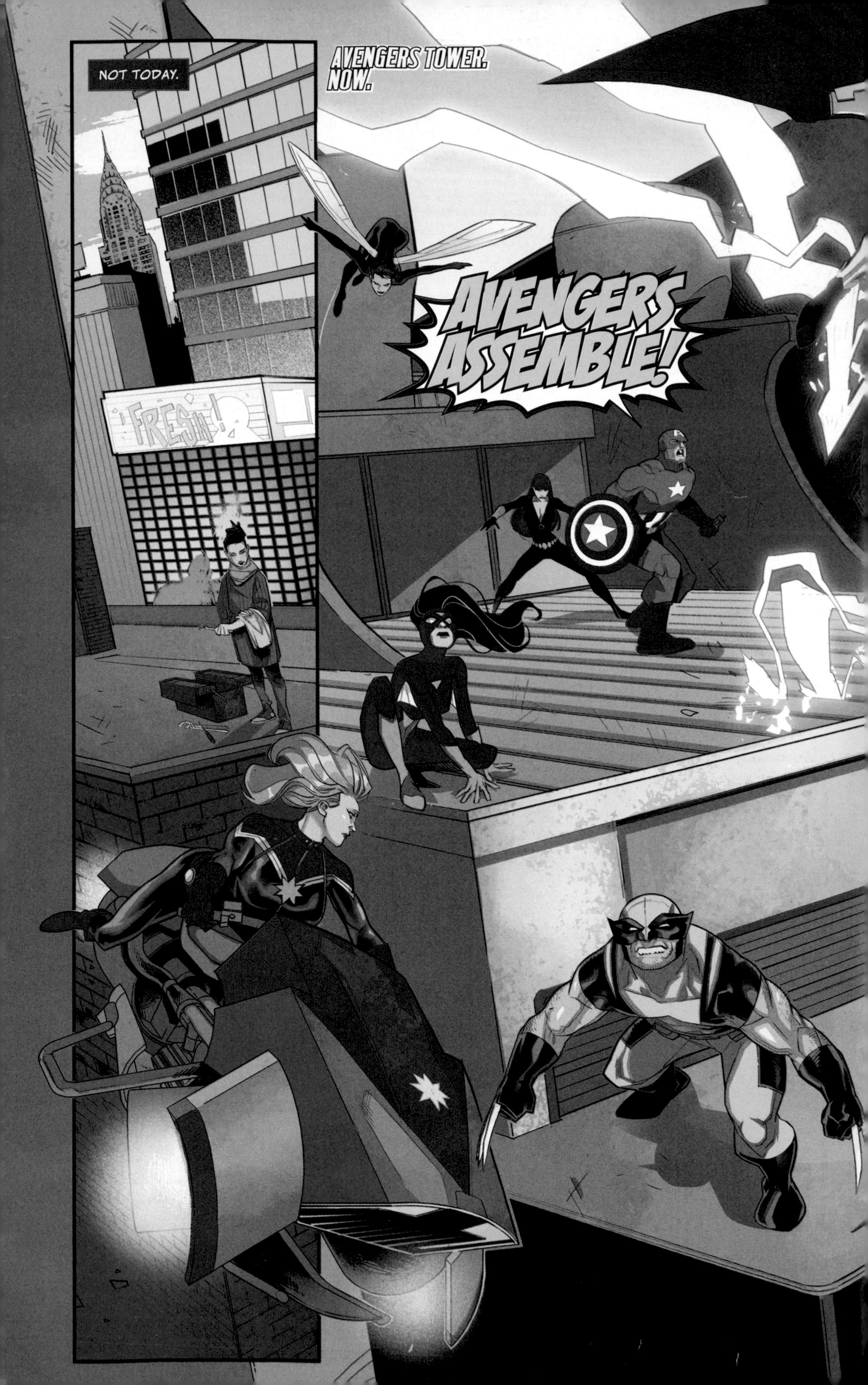
NOT TODAY.
FRESH!
AVENGERS TOWER. NOW.
AVENGERS ASSEMBLE!

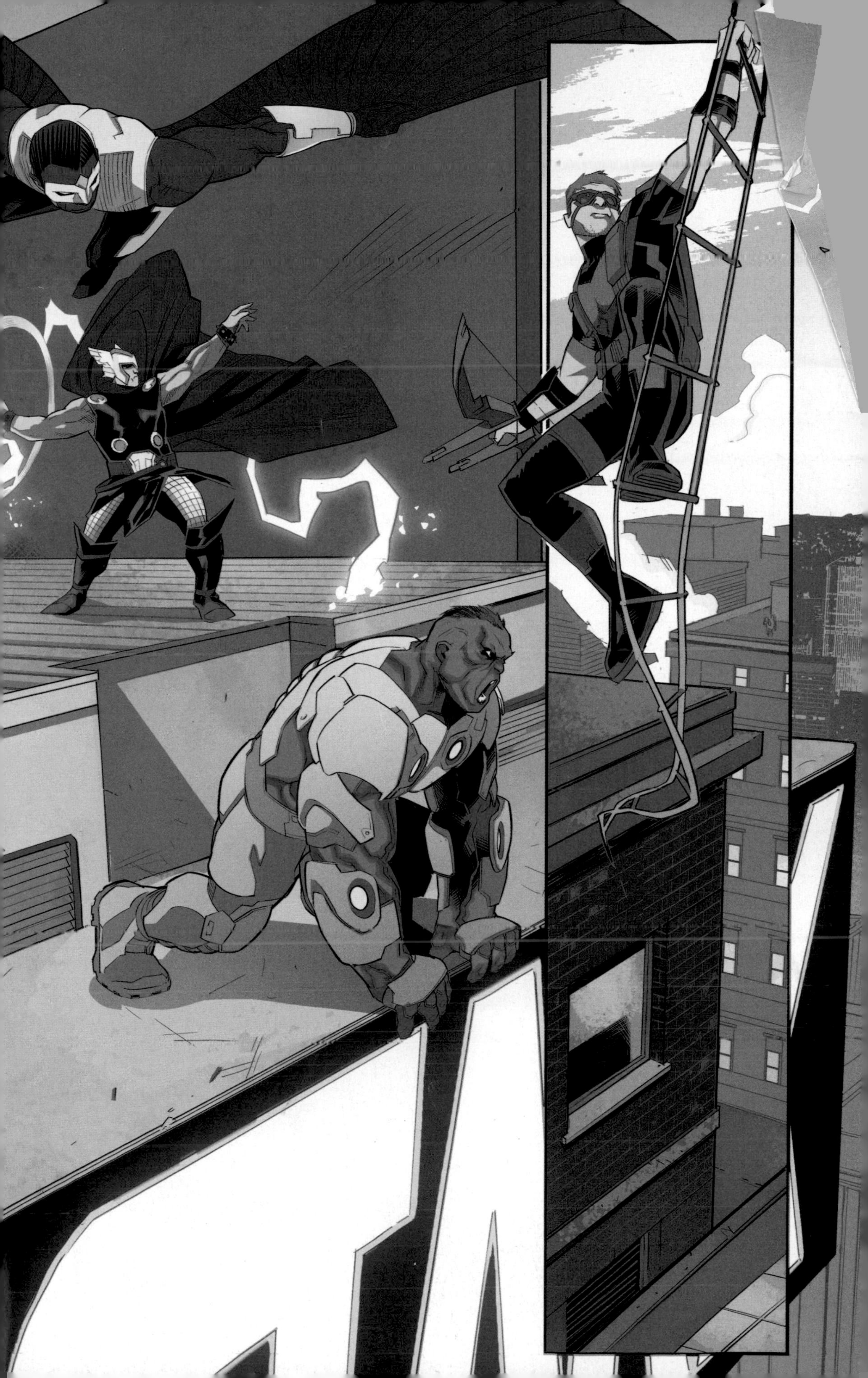

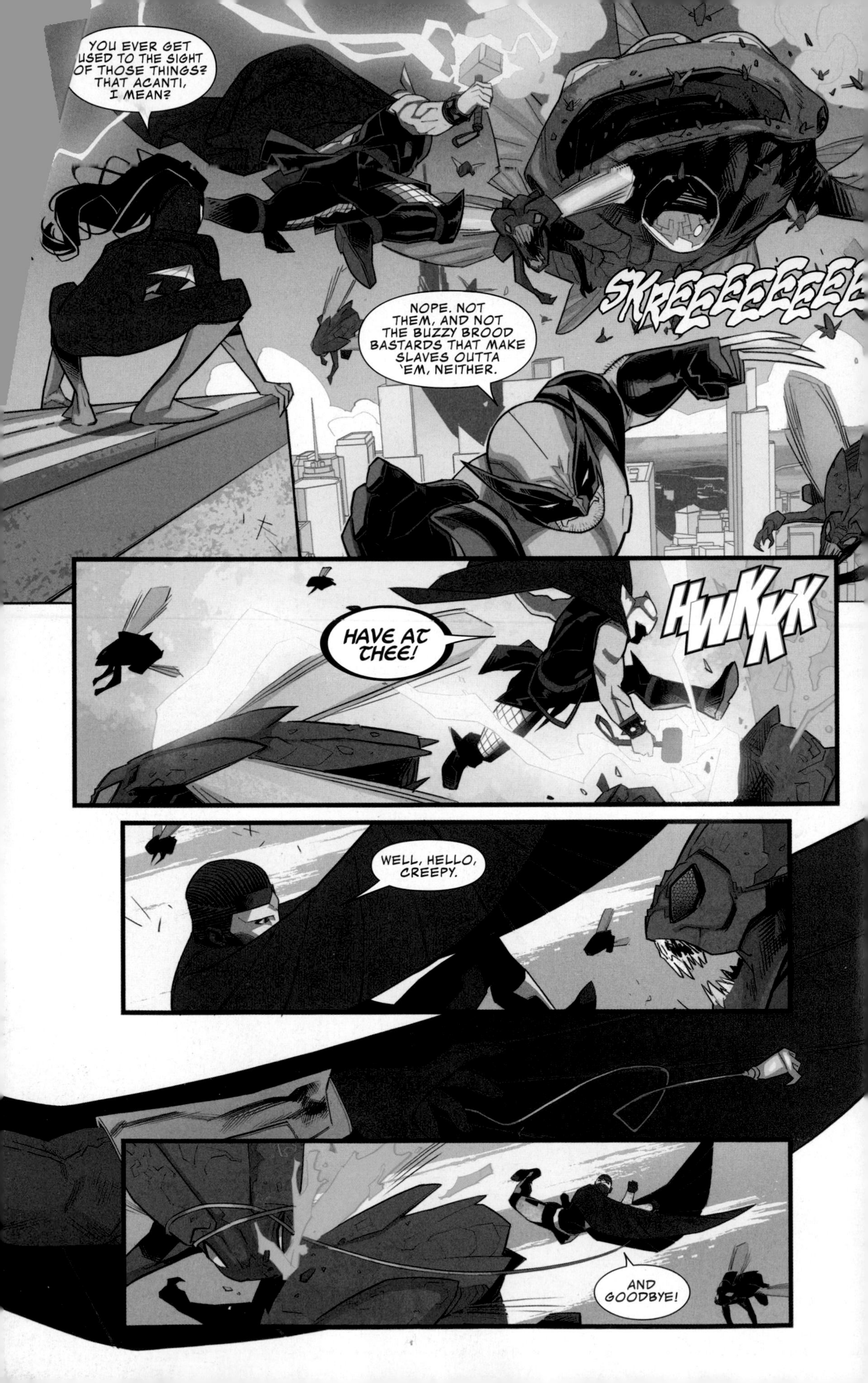
YOU EVER GET USED TO THE SIGHT OF THOSE THINGS? THAT ACANTI, I MEAN?
SKREEEEEEEEEE
NOPE. NOT THEM, AND NOT THE BUZZY BROOD BASTARDS THAT MAKE SLAVES OUTTA 'EM, NEITHER.
HAVE AT THEE!
HWKKK
WELL, HELLO, CREEPY.
AND GOODBYE!

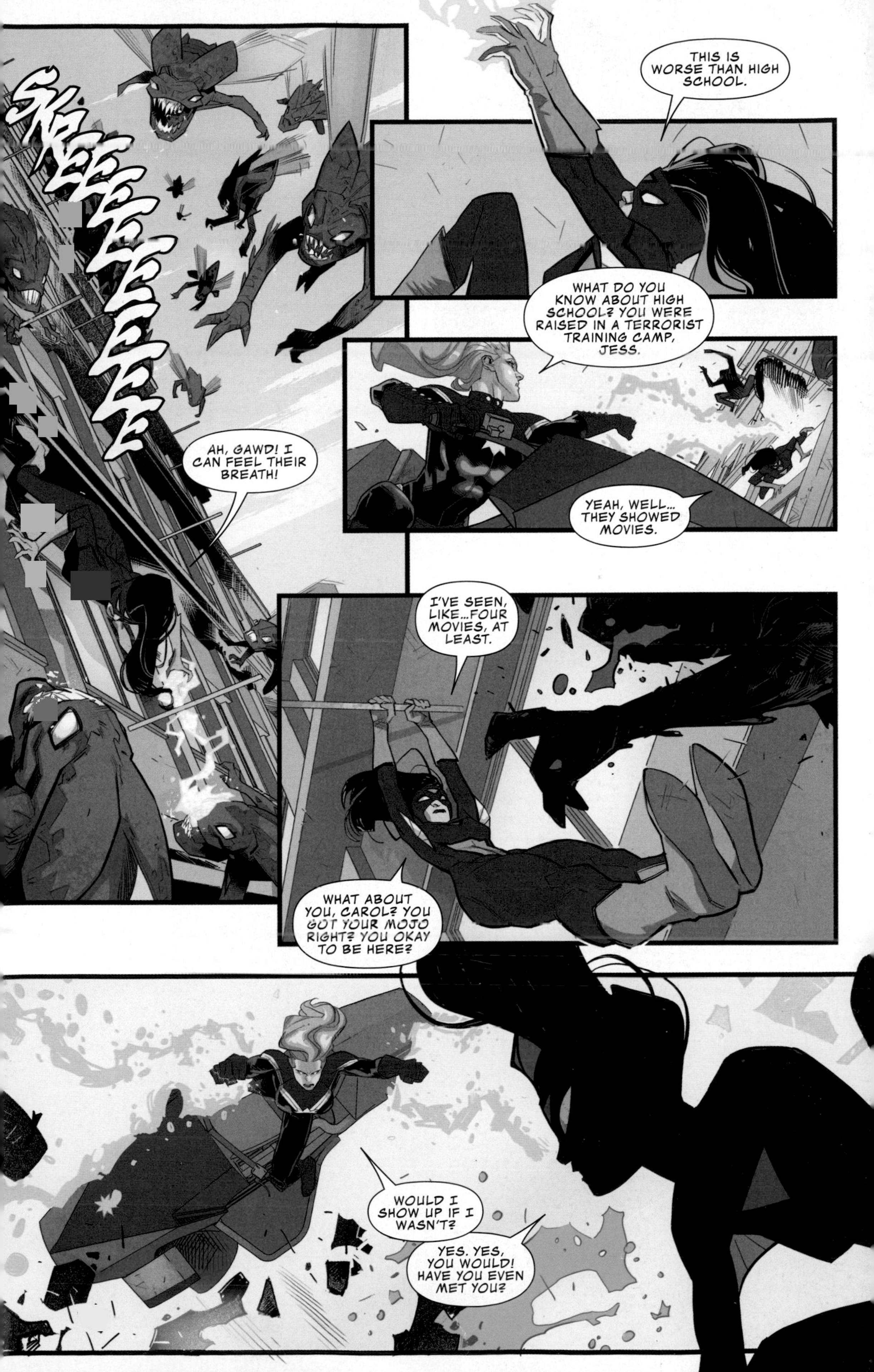
THIS IS WORSE THAN HIGH SCHOOL.
AH, GAWD! I CAN FEEL THEIR BREATH!
WHAT DO YOU KNOW ABOUT HIGH SCHOOL? YOU WERE RAISED IN A TERRORIST TRAINING CAMP, JESS.
YEAH, WELL... THEY SHOWED MOVIES.
I'VE SEEN, LIKE...FOUR MOVIES, AT LEAST.
WHAT ABOUT YOU, CAROL? YOU GOT YOUR MOJO RIGHT? YOU OKAY TO BE HERE?
WOULD I SHOW UP IF I WASN'T?
YES. YES, YOU WOULD! HAVE YOU EVEN MET YOU?

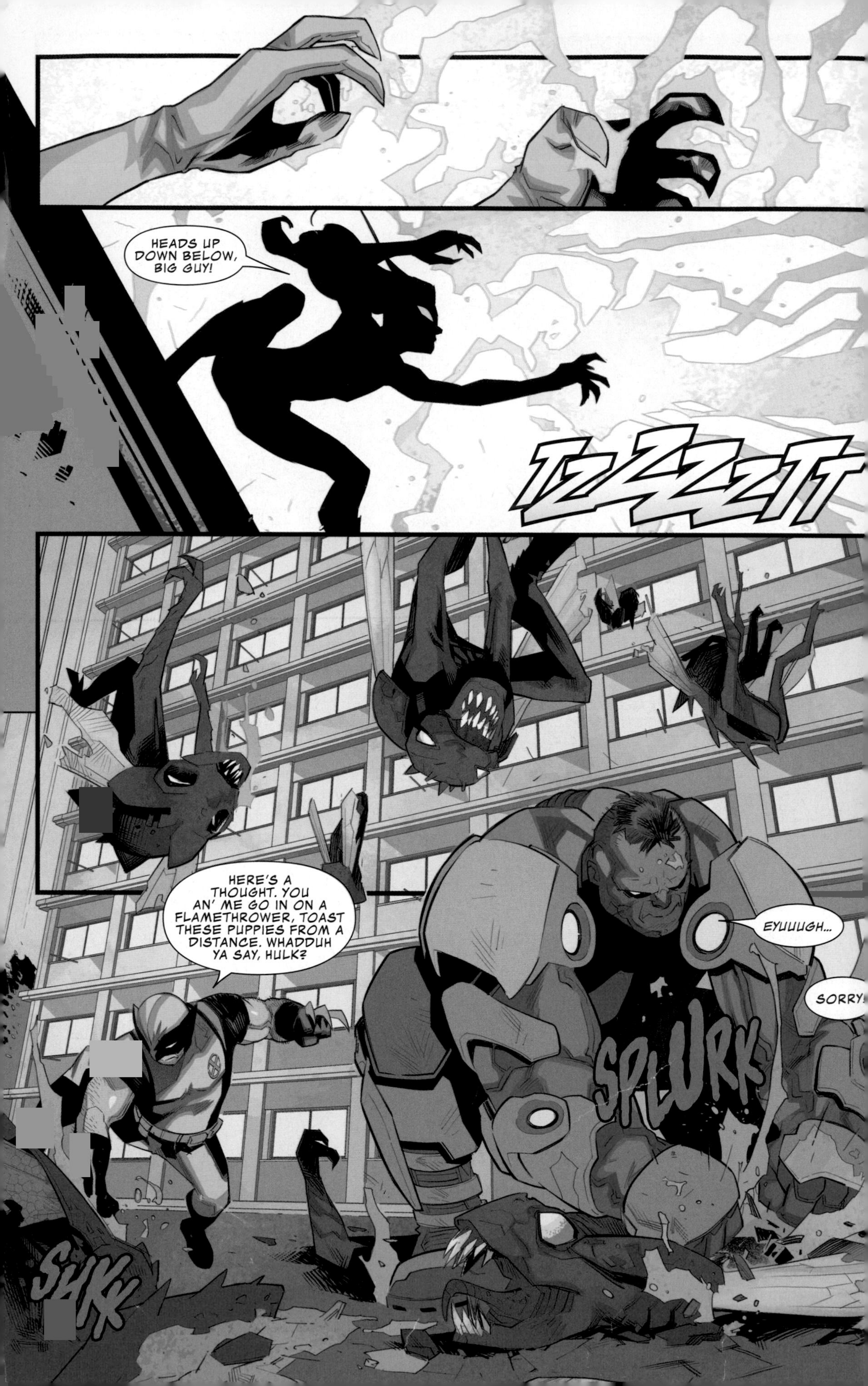
HEADS UP DOWN BELOW, BIG GUY!
TZZZZTT
HERE'S A THOUGHT. YOU AN' ME GO IN ON A FLAMETHROWER, TOAST THESE PUPPIES FROM A DISTANCE. WHADDUH YA SAY, HULK?
EYUUUGH...
SORRY!
SPLURK
SHKK

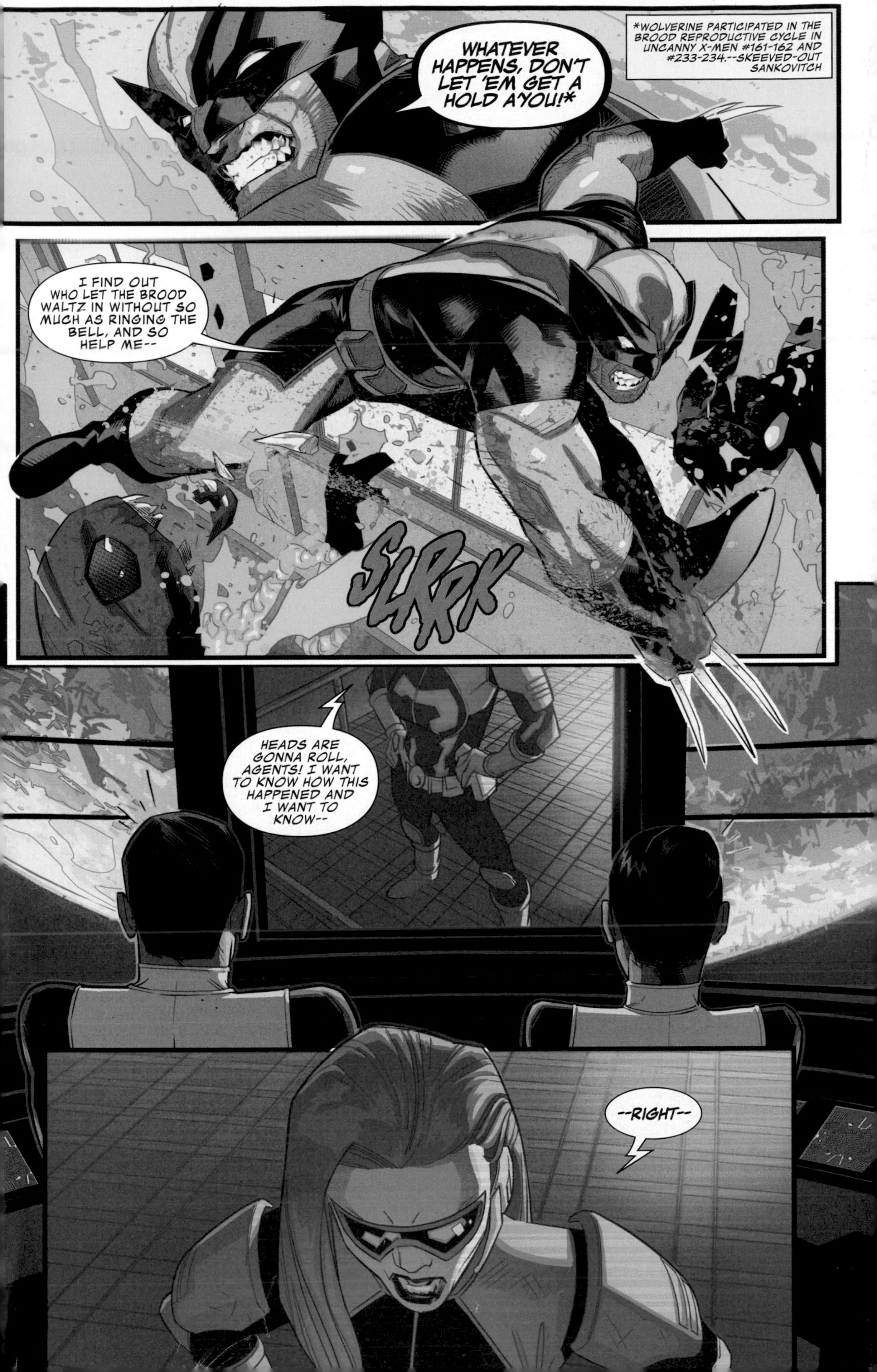

WHATEVER HAPPENS, DON'T LET 'EM GET A HOLD A'YOU!*
*WOLVERINE PARTICIPATED IN THE BROOD REPRODUCTIVE CYCLE IN UNCANNY X-MEN #161-162 AND #233-234.--SKEEVED-OUT SANKOVITCH
I FIND OUT WHO LET THE BROOD WALTZ IN WITHOUT SO MUCH AS RINGING THE BELL, AND SO HELP ME--
SLRRK
HEADS ARE GONNA ROLL, AGENTS! I WANT TO KNOW HOW THIS HAPPENED AND I WANT TO KNOW--
--RIGHT--

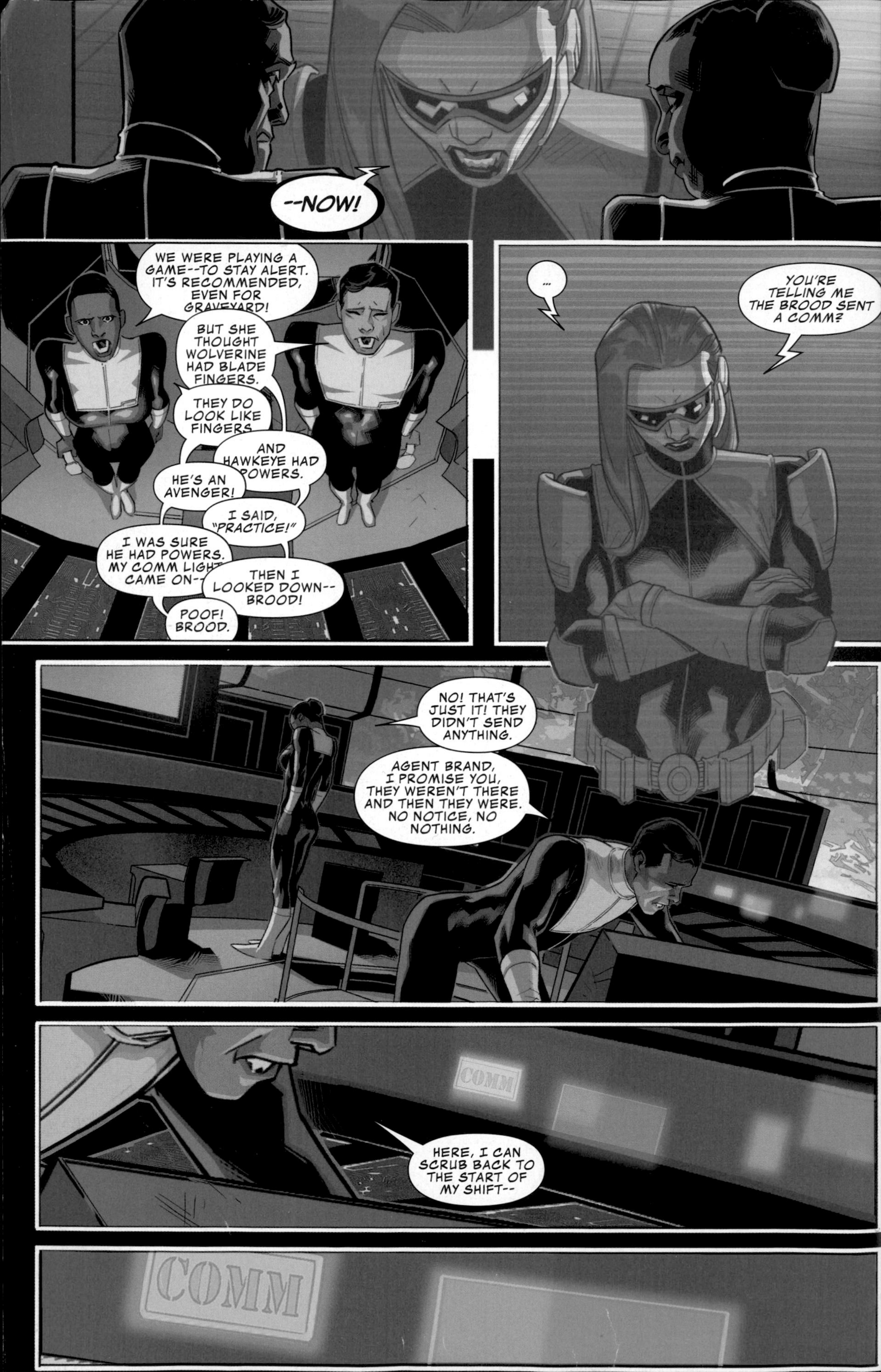
--NOW!
WE WERE PLAYING A GAME--TO STAY ALERT. IT'S RECOMMENDED, EVEN FOR GRAVEYARD!
BUT SHE THOUGHT WOLVERINE HAD BLADE FINGERS.
THEY DO LOOK LIKE FINGERS.
AND HAWKEYE HAD POWERS.
HE'S AN AVENGER!
I SAID, "PRACTICE!"
I WAS SURE HE HAD POWERS. MY COMM LIGHT CAME ON--
THEN I LOOKED DOWN--BROOD!
POOF! BROOD.
...
YOU'RE TELLING ME THE BROOD SENT A COMM?
NO! THAT'S JUST IT! THEY DIDN'T SEND ANYTHING.
AGENT BRAND, I PROMISE YOU, THEY WEREN'T THERE AND THEN THEY WERE. NO NOTICE, NO NOTHING.
COMM
HERE, I CAN SCRUB BACK TO THE START OF MY SHIFT--
COMM

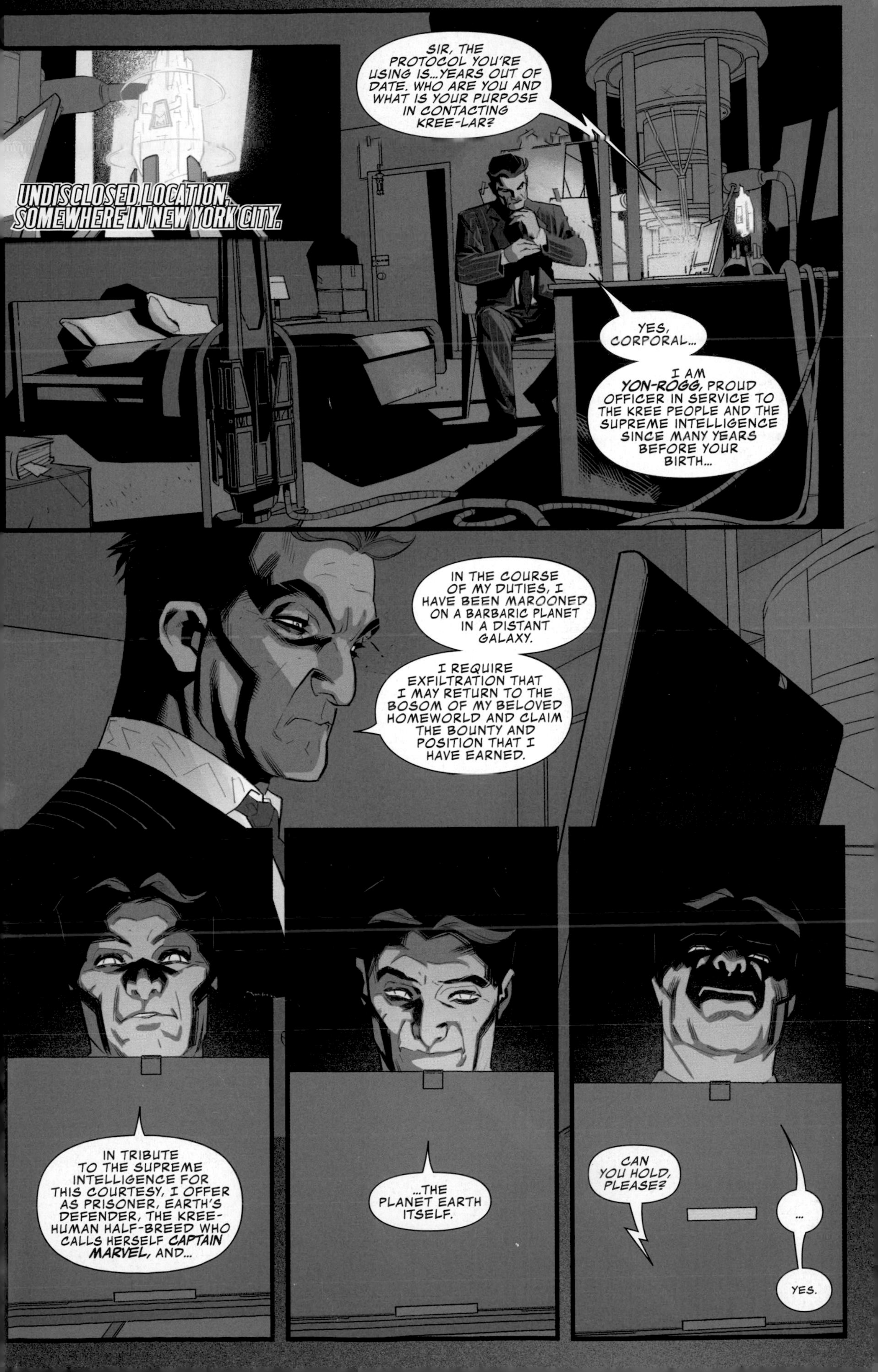

UNDISCLOSED LOCATION, SOMEWHERE IN NEW YORK CITY.
SIR, THE PROTOCOL YOU'RE USING IS...YEARS OUT OF DATE. WHO ARE YOU AND WHAT IS YOUR PURPOSE IN CONTACTING KREE-LAR?
YES, CORPORAL...
I AM YON-ROGG, PROUD OFFICER IN SERVICE TO THE KREE PEOPLE AND THE SUPREME INTELLIGENCE SINCE MANY YEARS BEFORE YOUR BIRTH...
IN THE COURSE OF MY DUTIES, I HAVE BEEN MAROONED ON A BARBARIC PLANET IN A DISTANT GALAXY.
I REQUIRE EXFILTRATION THAT I MAY RETURN TO THE BOSOM OF MY BELOVED HOMEWORLD AND CLAIM THE BOUNTY AND POSITION THAT I HAVE EARNED.
IN TRIBUTE TO THE SUPREME INTELLIGENCE FOR THIS COURTESY, I OFFER AS PRISONER, EARTH'S DEFENDER, THE KREE-HUMAN HALF-BREED WHO CALLS HERSELF CAPTAIN MARVEL, AND...
...THE PLANET EARTH ITSELF.
CAN YOU HOLD, PLEASE?
...
YES.

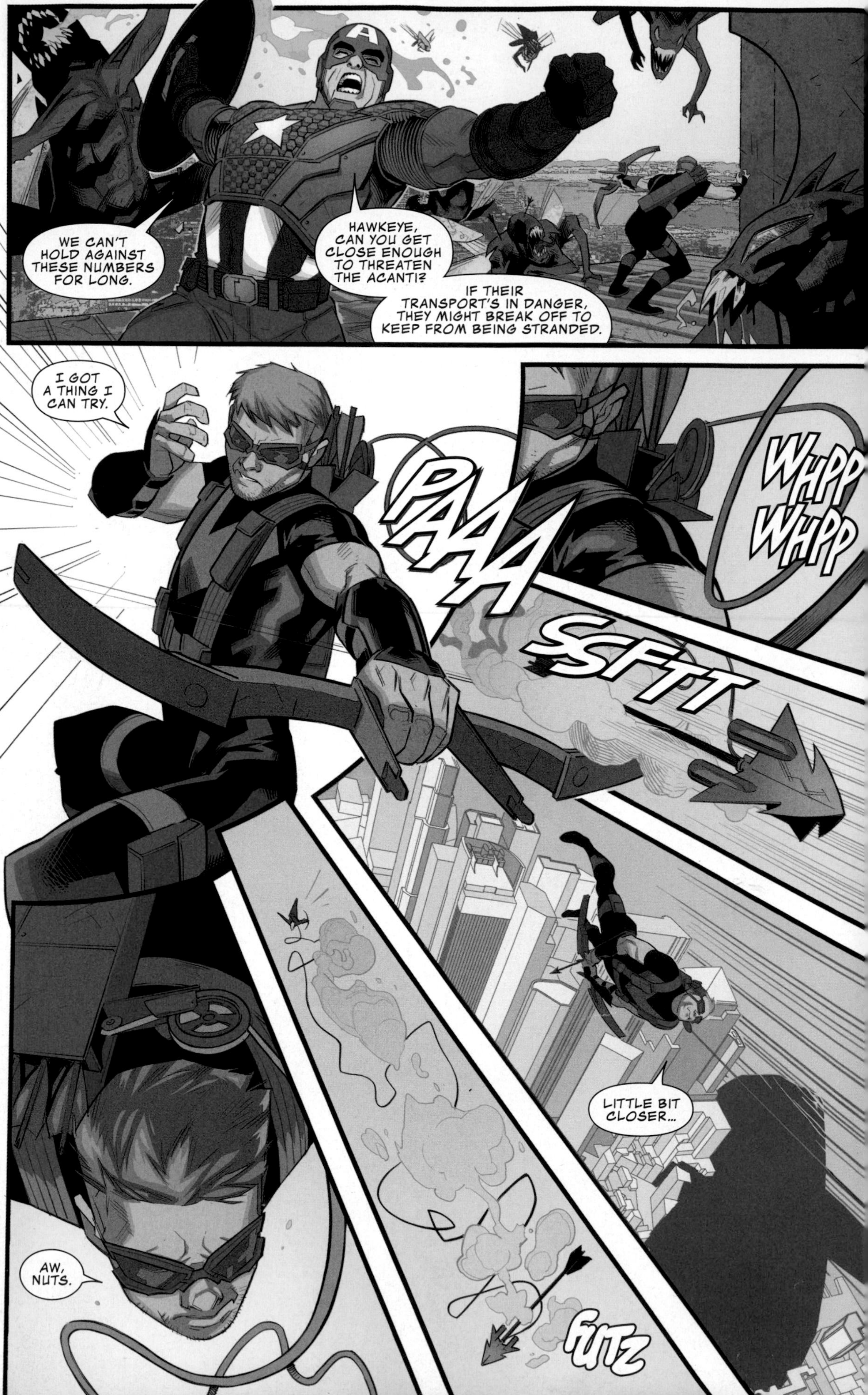
WE CAN'T HOLD AGAINST THESE NUMBERS FOR LONG.
HAWKEYE, CAN YOU GET CLOSE ENOUGH TO THREATEN THE ACANTI?
IF THEIR TRANSPORT'S IN DANGER, THEY MIGHT BREAK OFF TO KEEP FROM BEING STRANDED.
I GOT A THING I CAN TRY.
PAAA
WHPP WHPP
SSFTT
LITTLE BIT CLOSER...
AW, NUTS.
FUTZ

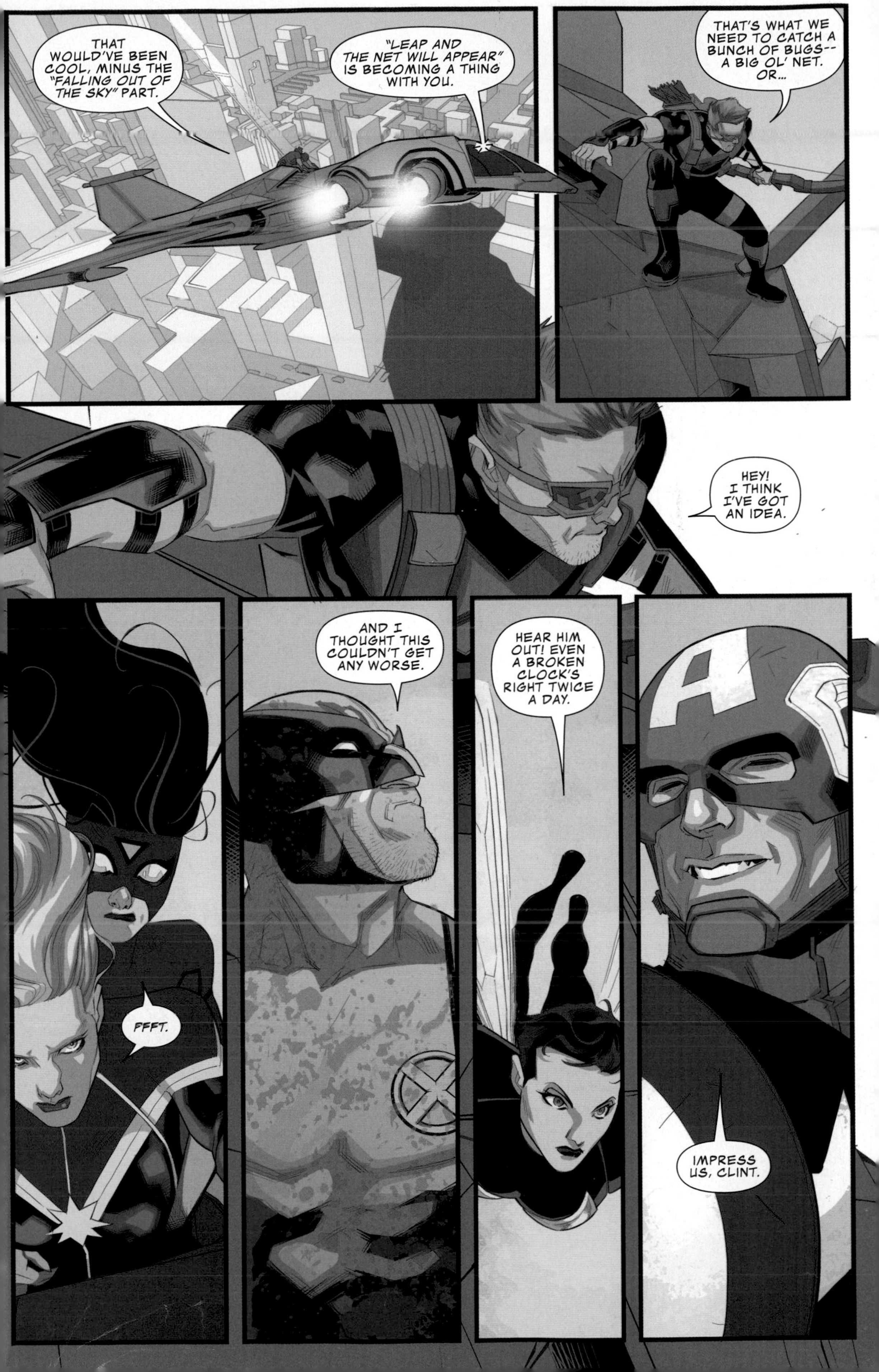
THAT WOULD'VE BEEN COOL, MINUS THE "FALLING OUT OF THE SKY" PART.
"LEAP AND THE NET WILL APPEAR" IS BECOMING A THING WITH YOU.
THAT'S WHAT WE NEED TO CATCH A BUNCH OF BUGS-- A BIG OL' NET. OR...
HEY! I THINK I'VE GOT AN IDEA.
PFFT.
AND I THOUGHT THIS COULDN'T GET ANY WORSE.
HEAR HIM OUT! EVEN A BROKEN CLOCK'S RIGHT TWICE A DAY.
IMPRESS US, CLINT.

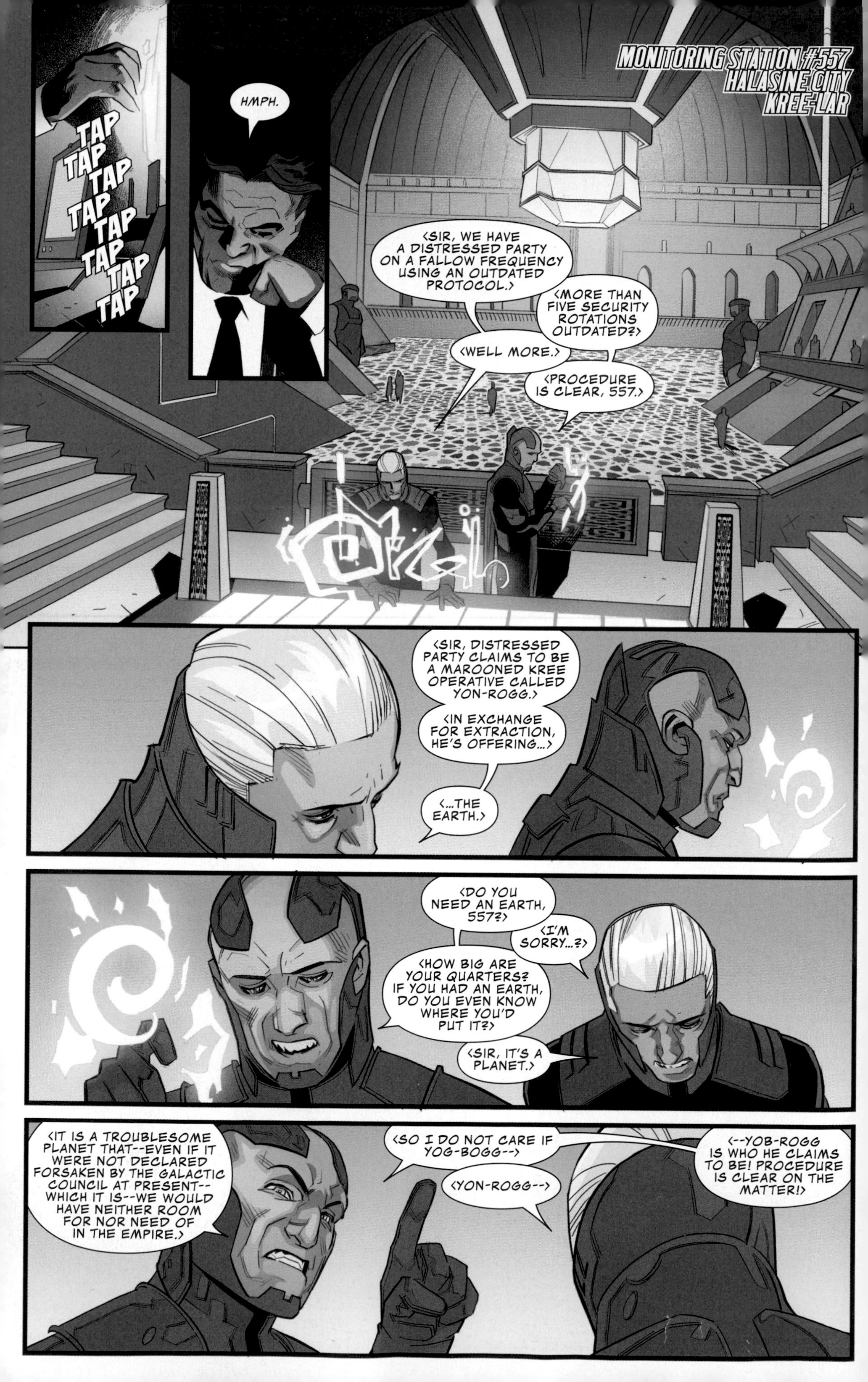
MONITORING STATION #557
HALASINE CITY
KREE-LAR
TAP TAP TAP TAP TAP TAP TAP TAP
HMPH.
<SIR, WE HAVE A DISTRESSED PARTY ON A FALLOW FREQUENCY USING AN OUTDATED PROTOCOL.>
<MORE THAN FIVE SECURITY ROTATIONS OUTDATED?>
<WELL MORE.>
<PROCEDURE IS CLEAR, 557.>
<SIR, DISTRESSED PARTY CLAIMS TO BE A MAROONED KREE OPERATIVE CALLED YON-ROGG.>
<IN EXCHANGE FOR EXTRACTION, HE'S OFFERING...>
<...THE EARTH.>
<DO YOU NEED AN EARTH, 557?>
<I'M SORRY...?>
<HOW BIG ARE YOUR QUARTERS? IF YOU HAD AN EARTH, DO YOU EVEN KNOW WHERE YOU'D PUT IT?>
<SIR, IT'S A PLANET.>
<IT IS A TROUBLESOME PLANET THAT--EVEN IF IT WERE NOT DECLARED FORSAKEN BY THE GALACTIC COUNCIL AT PRESENT--WHICH IT IS--WE WOULD HAVE NEITHER ROOM FOR NOR NEED OF IN THE EMPIRE.>
<SO I DO NOT CARE IF YOG-BOGG-->
<YON-ROGG-->
<--YOB-ROGG IS WHO HE CLAIMS TO BE! PROCEDURE IS CLEAR ON THE MATTER!>

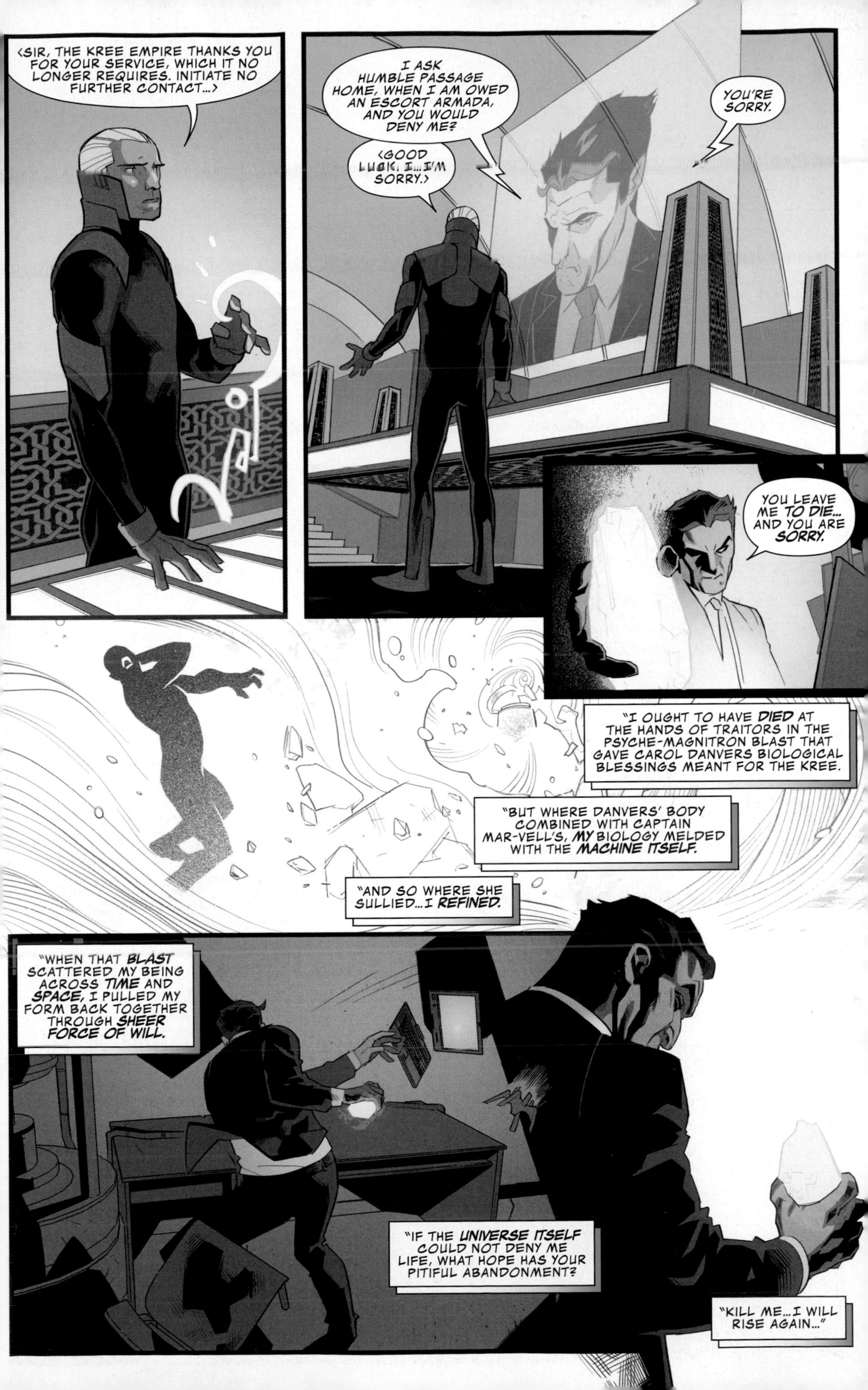

<SIR, THE KREE EMPIRE THANKS YOU FOR YOUR SERVICE, WHICH IT NO LONGER REQUIRES. INITIATE NO FURTHER CONTACT...>
I ASK HUMBLE PASSAGE HOME, WHEN I AM OWED AN ESCORT ARMADA, AND YOU WOULD DENY ME?
<GOOD LUCK. I...I'M SORRY.>
YOU'RE SORRY.
YOU LEAVE ME TO DIE... AND YOU ARE SORRY.
"I OUGHT TO HAVE DIED AT THE HANDS OF TRAITORS IN THE PSYCHE-MAGNITRON BLAST THAT GAVE CAROL DANVERS BIOLOGICAL BLESSINGS MEANT FOR THE KREE.
"BUT WHERE DANVERS' BODY COMBINED WITH CAPTAIN MAR-VELL'S, MY BIOLOGY MELDED WITH THE MACHINE ITSELF.
"AND SO WHERE SHE SULLIED...I REFINED.
"WHEN THAT BLAST SCATTERED MY BEING ACROSS TIME AND SPACE, I PULLED MY FORM BACK TOGETHER THROUGH SHEER FORCE OF WILL.
"IF THE UNIVERSE ITSELF COULD NOT DENY ME LIFE, WHAT HOPE HAS YOUR PITIFUL ABANDONMENT?
"KILL ME...I WILL RISE AGAIN..."

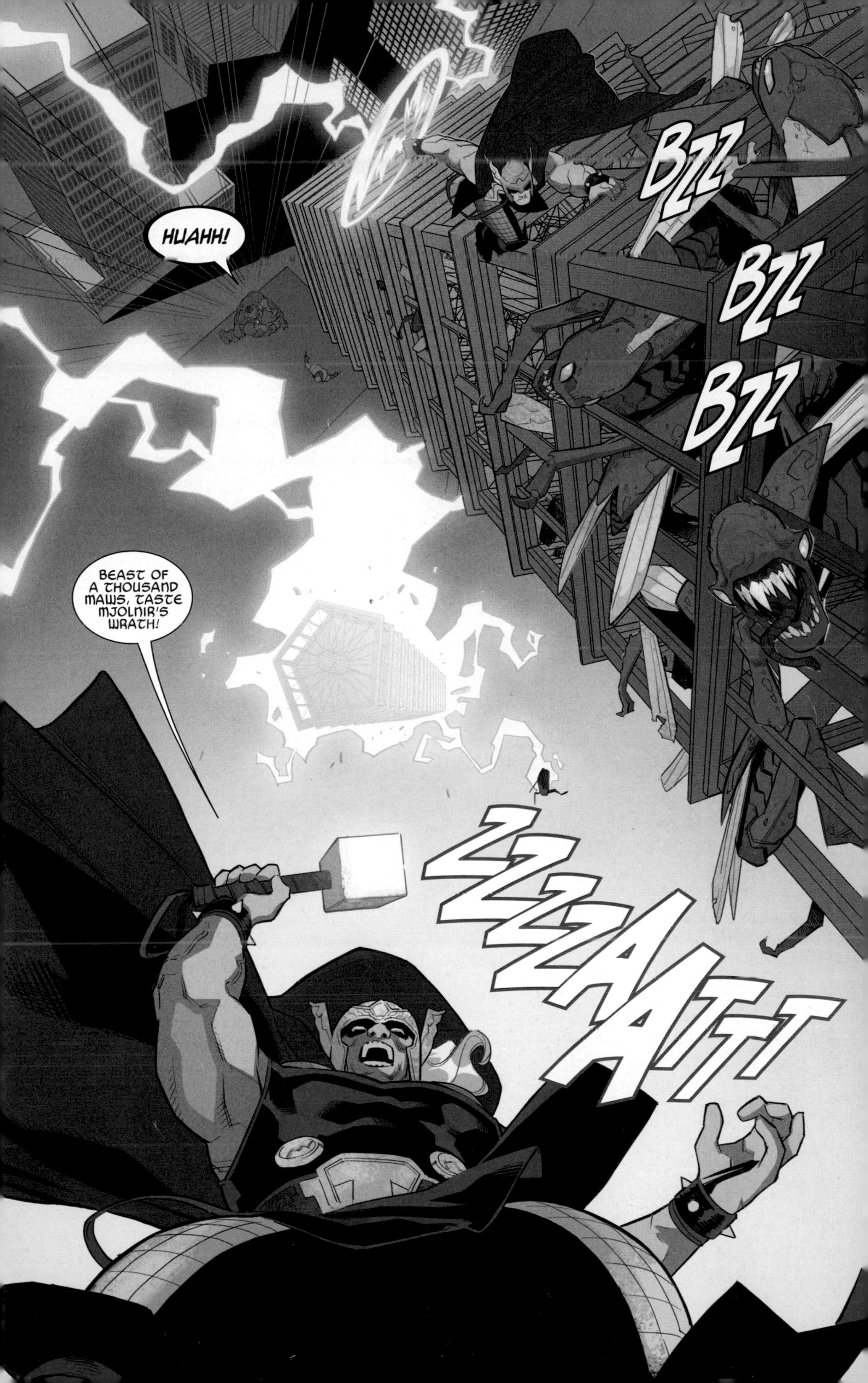
HUAHH!
BZZ
BZZ
BZZ
BEAST OF A THOUSAND MAWS, TASTE MJOLNIR'S WRATH!
ZZZZAATTT

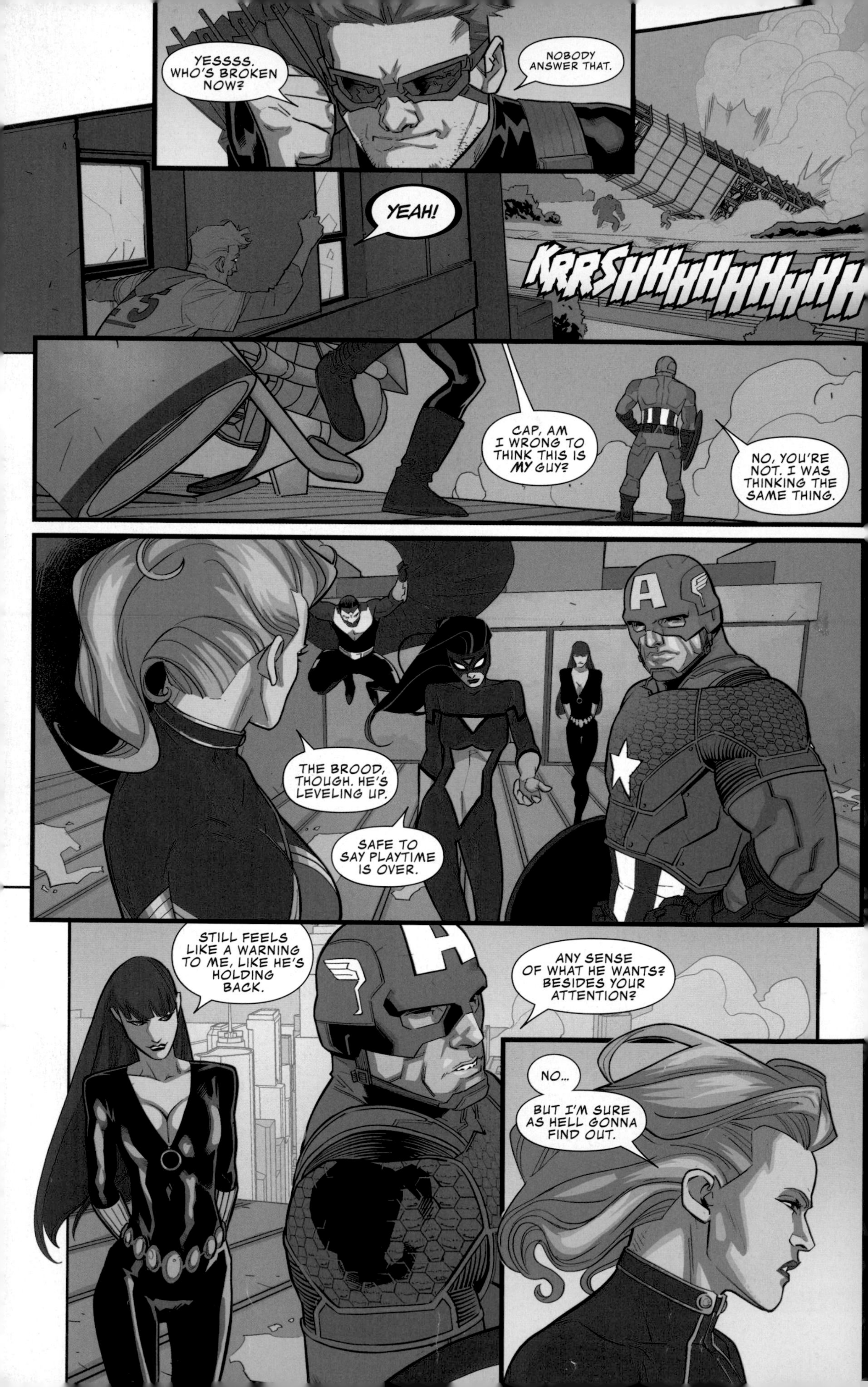
YESSSS. WHO'S BROKEN NOW?
NOBODY ANSWER THAT.
YEAH!
KRRSHHHHHHHHHHH
CAP, AM I WRONG TO THINK THIS IS MY GUY?
NO, YOU'RE NOT. I WAS THINKING THE SAME THING.
THE BROOD, THOUGH. HE'S LEVELING UP.
SAFE TO SAY PLAYTIME IS OVER.
STILL FEELS LIKE A WARNING TO ME, LIKE HE'S HOLDING BACK.
ANY SENSE OF WHAT HE WANTS? BESIDES YOUR ATTENTION?
NO...
BUT I'M SURE AS HELL GONNA FIND OUT.

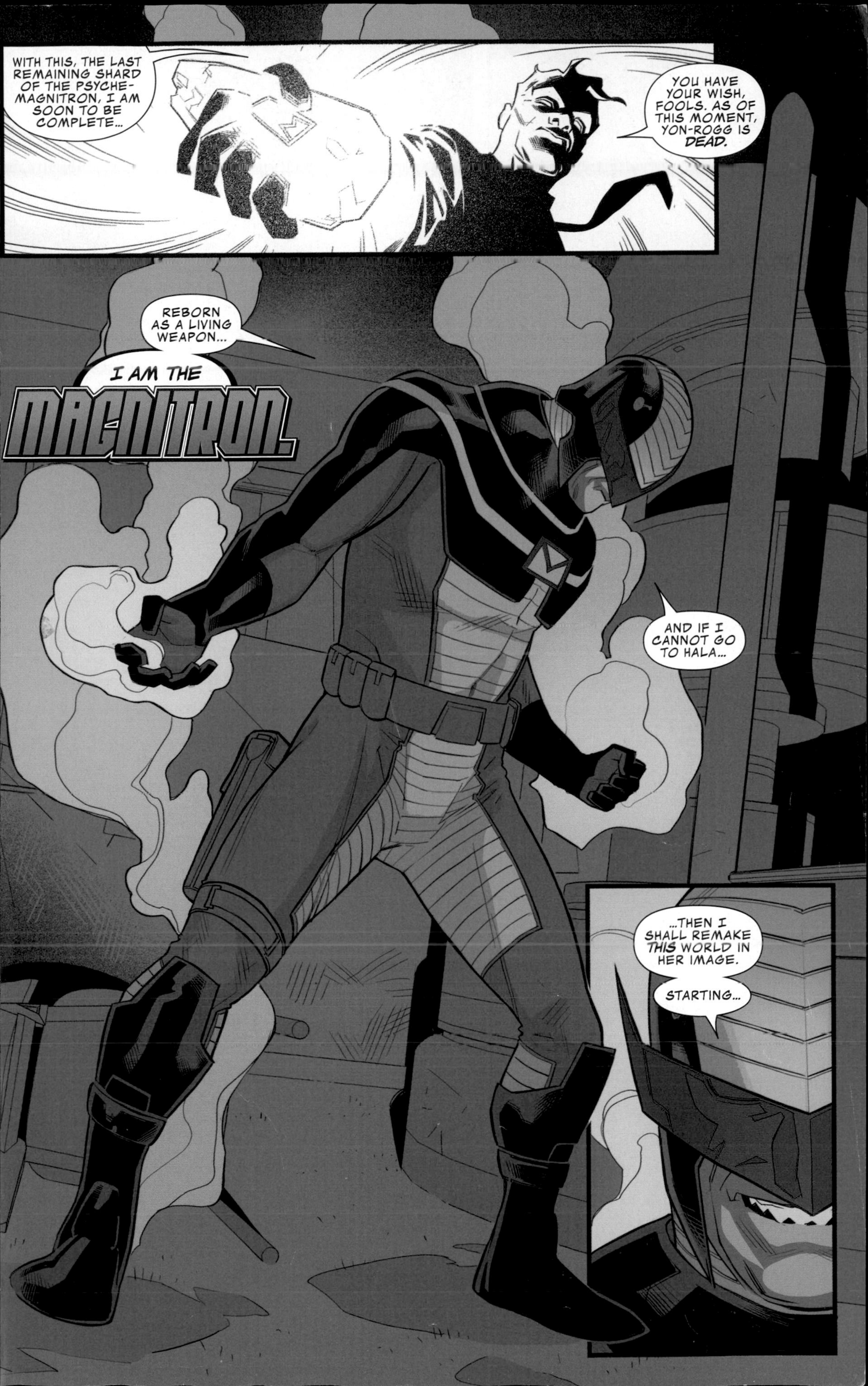
WITH THIS, THE LAST REMAINING SHARD OF THE PSYCHE-MAGNITRON, I AM SOON TO BE COMPLETE...
YOU HAVE YOUR WISH, FOOLS. AS OF THIS MOMENT, YON-ROGG IS *DEAD.*
REBORN AS A LIVING WEAPON...
I AM THE
MAGNITRON.
AND IF I CANNOT GO TO HALA...
...THEN I SHALL REMAKE *THIS* WORLD IN HER IMAGE.
STARTING...

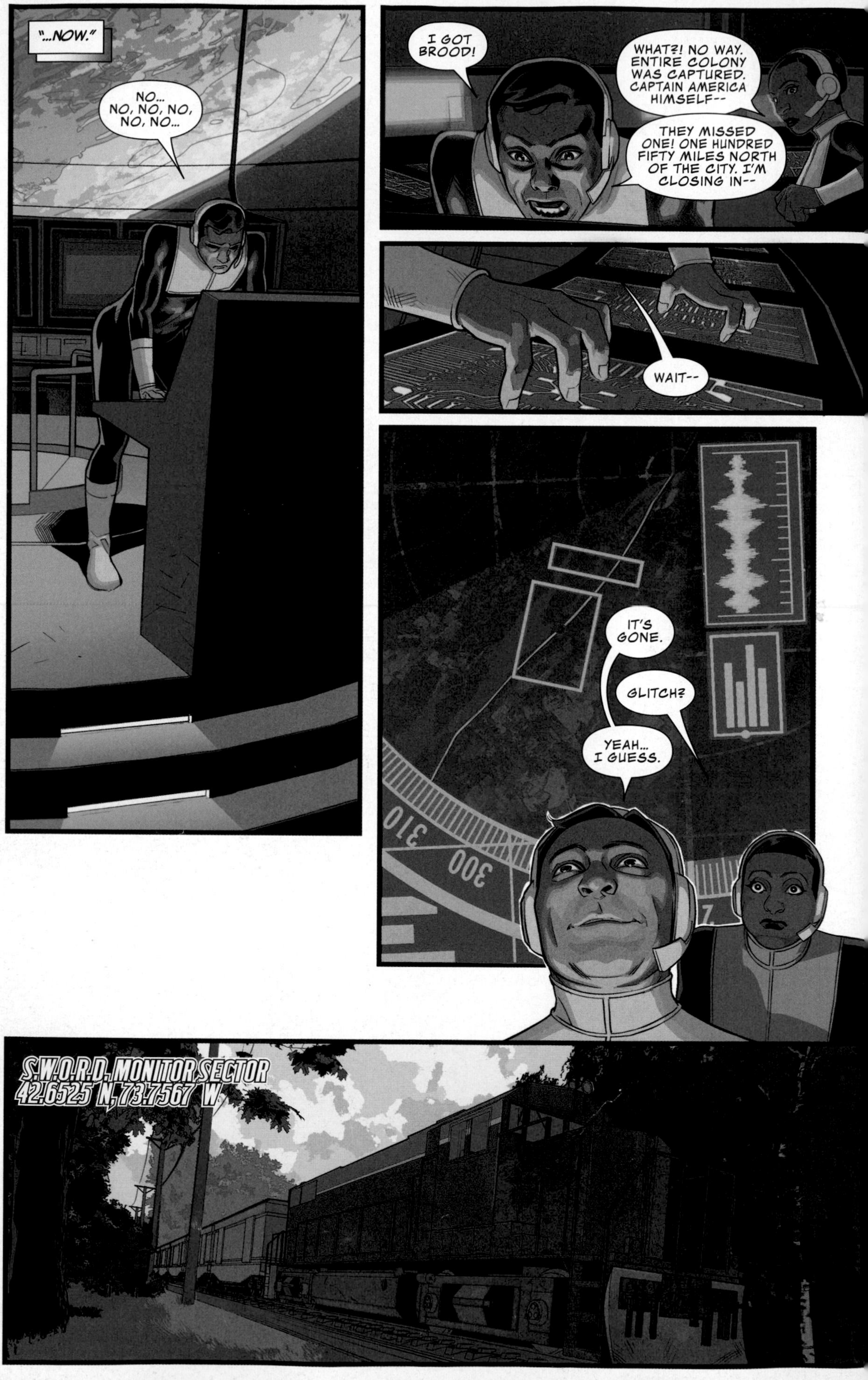
"...NOW."
NO... NO, NO, NO, NO, NO...
I GOT BROOD!
WHAT?! NO WAY. ENTIRE COLONY WAS CAPTURED. CAPTAIN AMERICA HIMSELF--
THEY MISSED ONE! ONE HUNDRED FIFTY MILES NORTH OF THE CITY. I'M CLOSING IN--
WAIT--
IT'S GONE.
GLITCH?
YEAH... I GUESS.
S.W.O.R.D. MONITOR SECTOR 42.6525 N, 73.7567 W

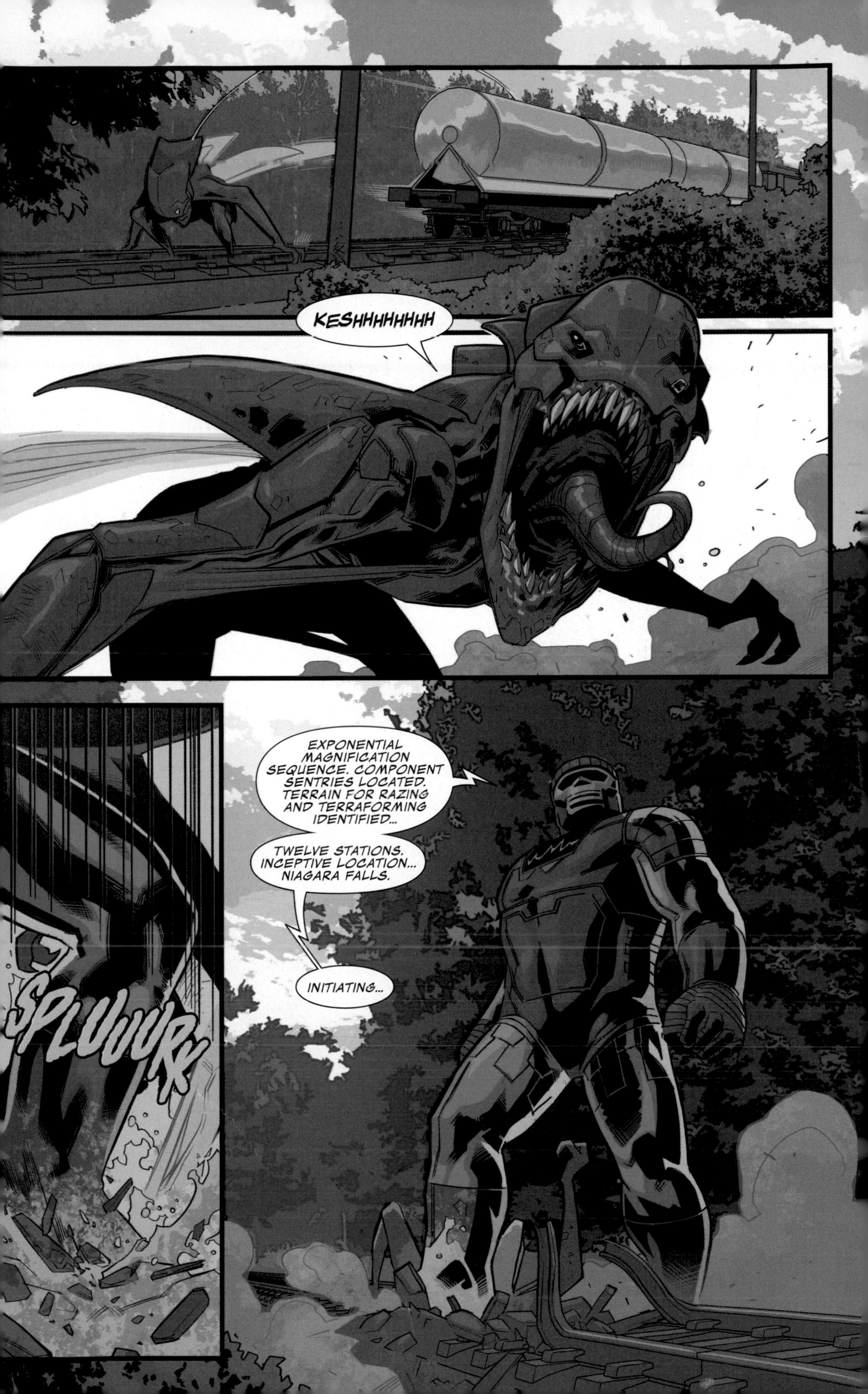
KESHHHHHHHH
EXPONENTIAL MAGNIFICATION SEQUENCE. COMPONENT SENTRIES LOCATED. TERRAIN FOR RAZING AND TERRAFORMING IDENTIFIED...
TWELVE STATIONS. INCEPTIVE LOCATION... NIAGARA FALLS.
INITIATING...
SPLUUURK

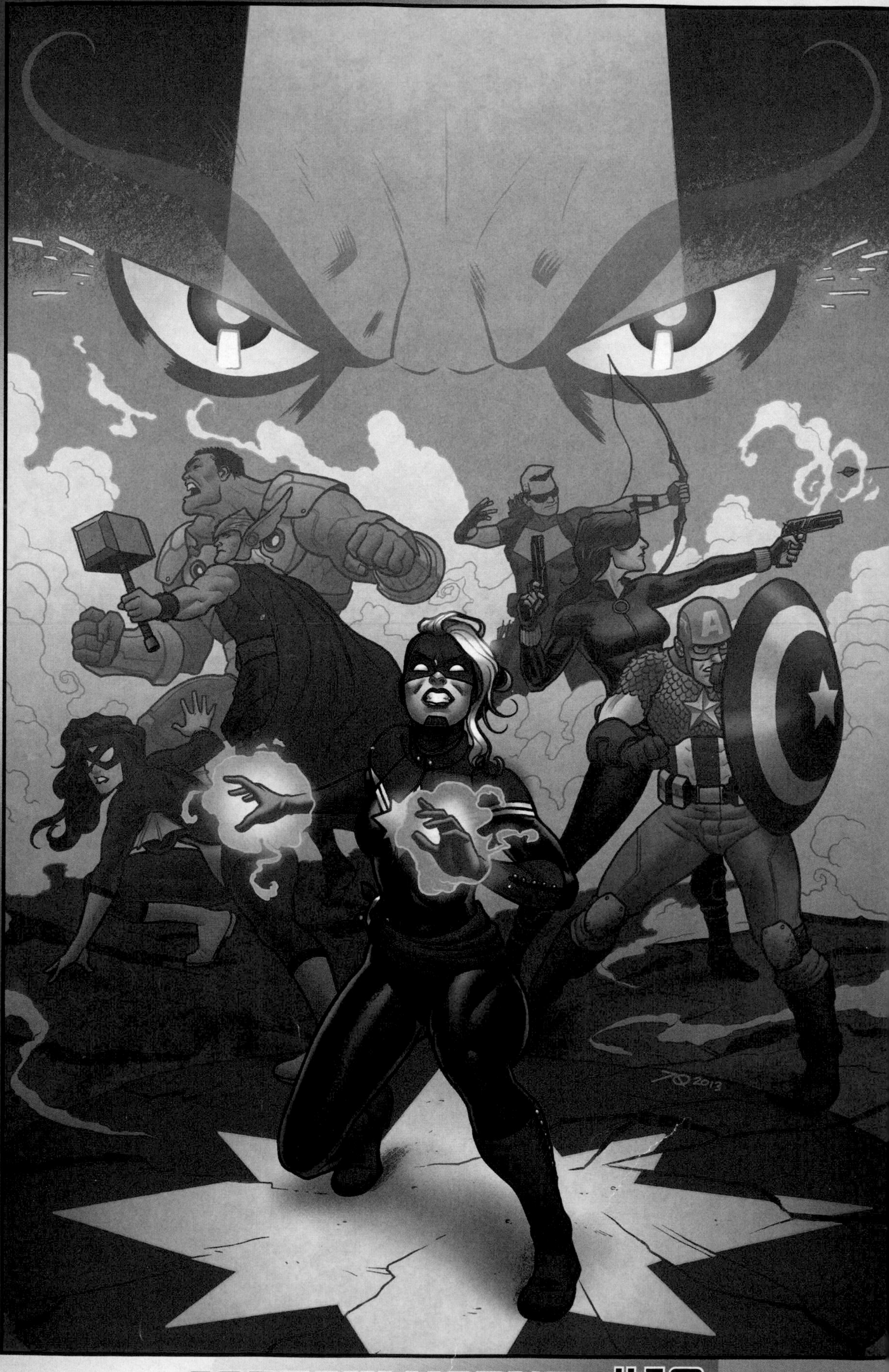

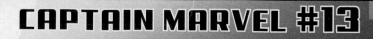

CAPTAIN MARVEL #13

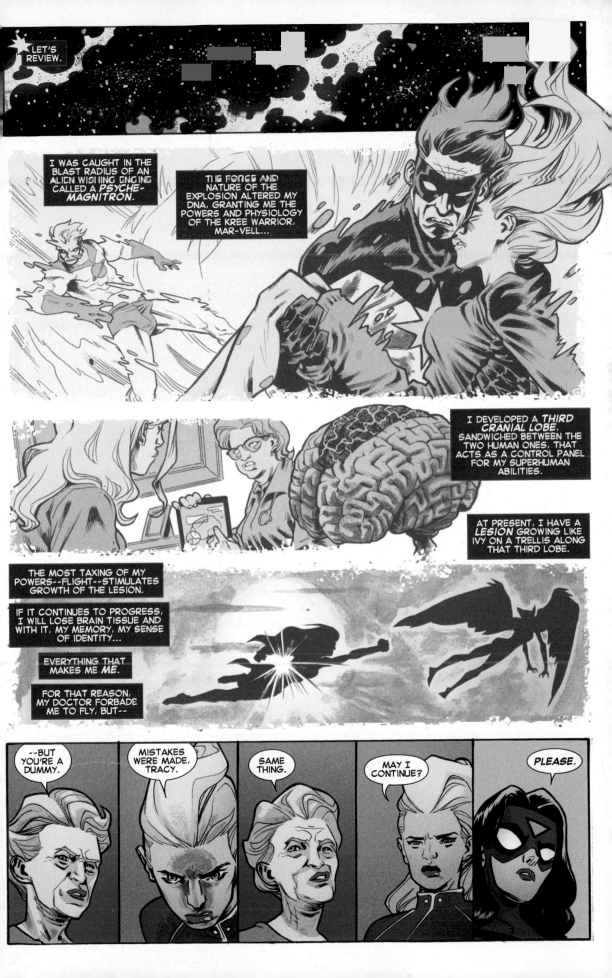

LET'S REVIEW.

I WAS CAUGHT IN THE BLAST RADIUS OF AN ALIEN WIGHING ENGINE CALLED A *PSYCHE-MAGNITRON.*

THE FORCE AND NATURE OF THE EXPLOSION ALTERED MY DNA, GRANTING ME THE POWERS AND PHYSIOLOGY OF THE KREE WARRIOR, MAR-VELL...

I DEVELOPED A *THIRD CRANIAL LOBE,* SANDWICHED BETWEEN THE TWO HUMAN ONES, THAT ACTS AS A CONTROL PANEL FOR MY SUPERHUMAN ABILITIES.

AT PRESENT, I HAVE A *LESION* GROWING LIKE IVY ON A TRELLIS ALONG THAT THIRD LOBE.

THE MOST TAXING OF MY POWERS--FLIGHT--STIMULATES GROWTH OF THE LESION.

IF IT CONTINUES TO PROGRESS, I WILL LOSE BRAIN TISSUE AND WITH IT, MY MEMORY, MY SENSE OF IDENTITY...

EVERYTHING THAT MAKES ME *ME.*

FOR THAT REASON, MY DOCTOR FORBADE ME TO FLY, BUT--

--BUT YOU'RE A DUMMY.

MISTAKES WERE MADE, TRACY.

SAME THING.

MAY I CONTINUE?

PLEASE.

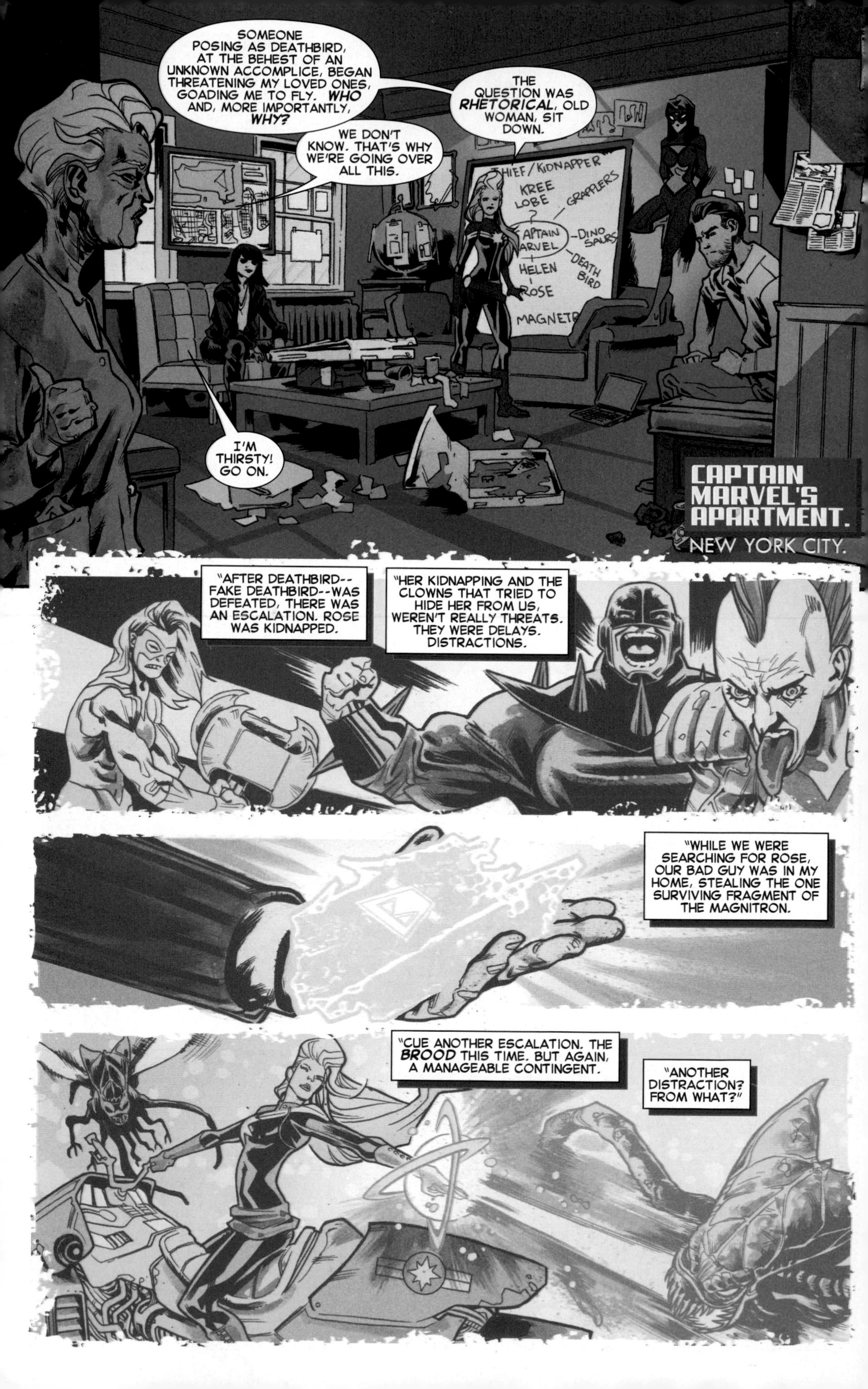
SOMEONE POSING AS DEATHBIRD, AT THE BEHEST OF AN UNKNOWN ACCOMPLICE, BEGAN THREATENING MY LOVED ONES, GOADING ME TO FLY. WHO AND, MORE IMPORTANTLY, WHY?
THE QUESTION WAS RHETORICAL, OLD WOMAN, SIT DOWN.
WE DON'T KNOW. THAT'S WHY WE'RE GOING OVER ALL THIS.
THIEF/KIDNAPPER
KREE LOBE
GRAPPLERS
CAPTAIN MARVEL
DINO SAURS
HELEN
DEATH BIRD
ROSE
MAGNETR
I'M THIRSTY! GO ON.
CAPTAIN MARVEL'S APARTMENT.
NEW YORK CITY.
"AFTER DEATHBIRD-- FAKE DEATHBIRD--WAS DEFEATED, THERE WAS AN ESCALATION. ROSE WAS KIDNAPPED.
"HER KIDNAPPING AND THE CLOWNS THAT TRIED TO HIDE HER FROM US, WEREN'T REALLY THREATS. THEY WERE DELAYS. DISTRACTIONS.
"WHILE WE WERE SEARCHING FOR ROSE, OUR BAD GUY WAS IN MY HOME, STEALING THE ONE SURVIVING FRAGMENT OF THE MAGNITRON.
"CUE ANOTHER ESCALATION. THE BROOD THIS TIME. BUT AGAIN, A MANAGEABLE CONTINGENT.
"ANOTHER DISTRACTION? FROM WHAT?"

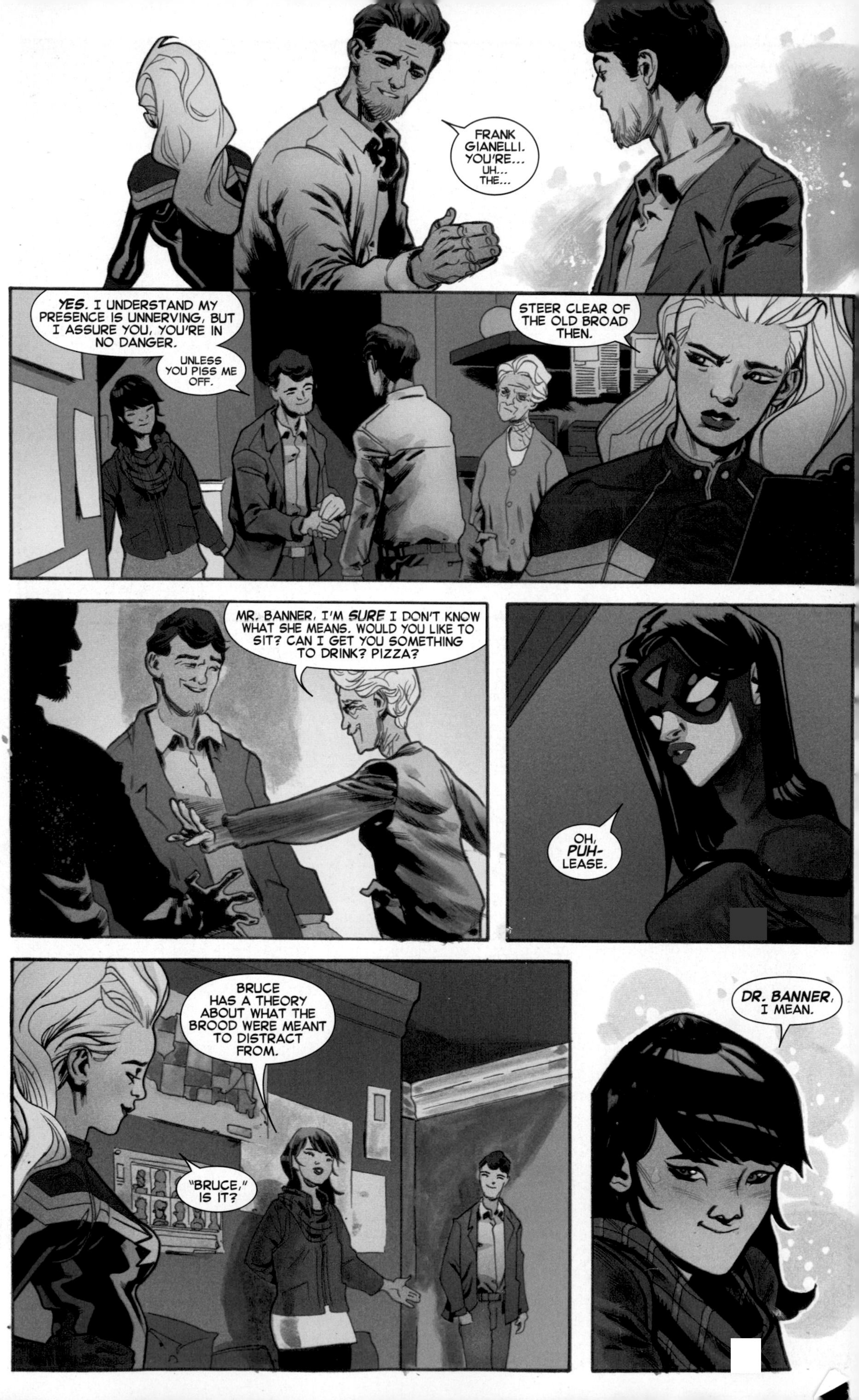
FRANK GIANELLI. YOU'RE... UH... THE...
YES. I UNDERSTAND MY PRESENCE IS UNNERVING, BUT I ASSURE YOU, YOU'RE IN NO DANGER.
UNLESS YOU PISS ME OFF.
STEER CLEAR OF THE OLD BROAD THEN.
MR. BANNER, I'M SURE I DON'T KNOW WHAT SHE MEANS. WOULD YOU LIKE TO SIT? CAN I GET YOU SOMETHING TO DRINK? PIZZA?
OH, PUH-LEASE.
BRUCE HAS A THEORY ABOUT WHAT THE BROOD WERE MEANT TO DISTRACT FROM.
"BRUCE," IS IT?
DR. BANNER, I MEAN.

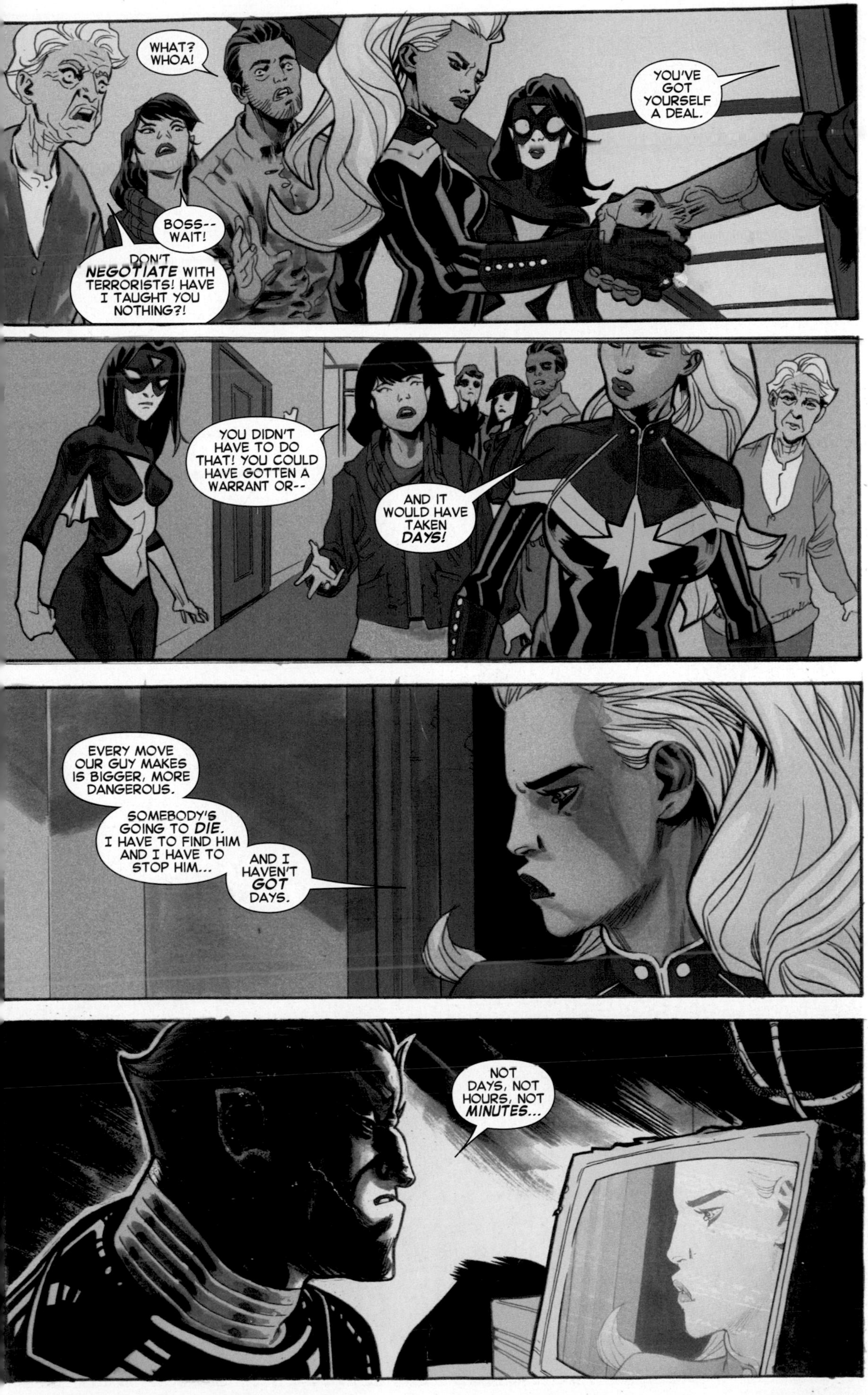
WHAT? WHOA!
YOU'VE GOT YOURSELF A DEAL.
BOSS-- WAIT!
DON'T NEGOTIATE WITH TERRORISTS! HAVE I TAUGHT YOU NOTHING?!
YOU DIDN'T HAVE TO DO THAT! YOU COULD HAVE GOTTEN A WARRANT OR--
AND IT WOULD HAVE TAKEN DAYS!
EVERY MOVE OUR GUY MAKES IS BIGGER, MORE DANGEROUS.
SOMEBODY'S GOING TO DIE. I HAVE TO FIND HIM AND I HAVE TO STOP HIM...
AND I HAVEN'T GOT DAYS.
NOT DAYS, NOT HOURS, NOT MINUTES...

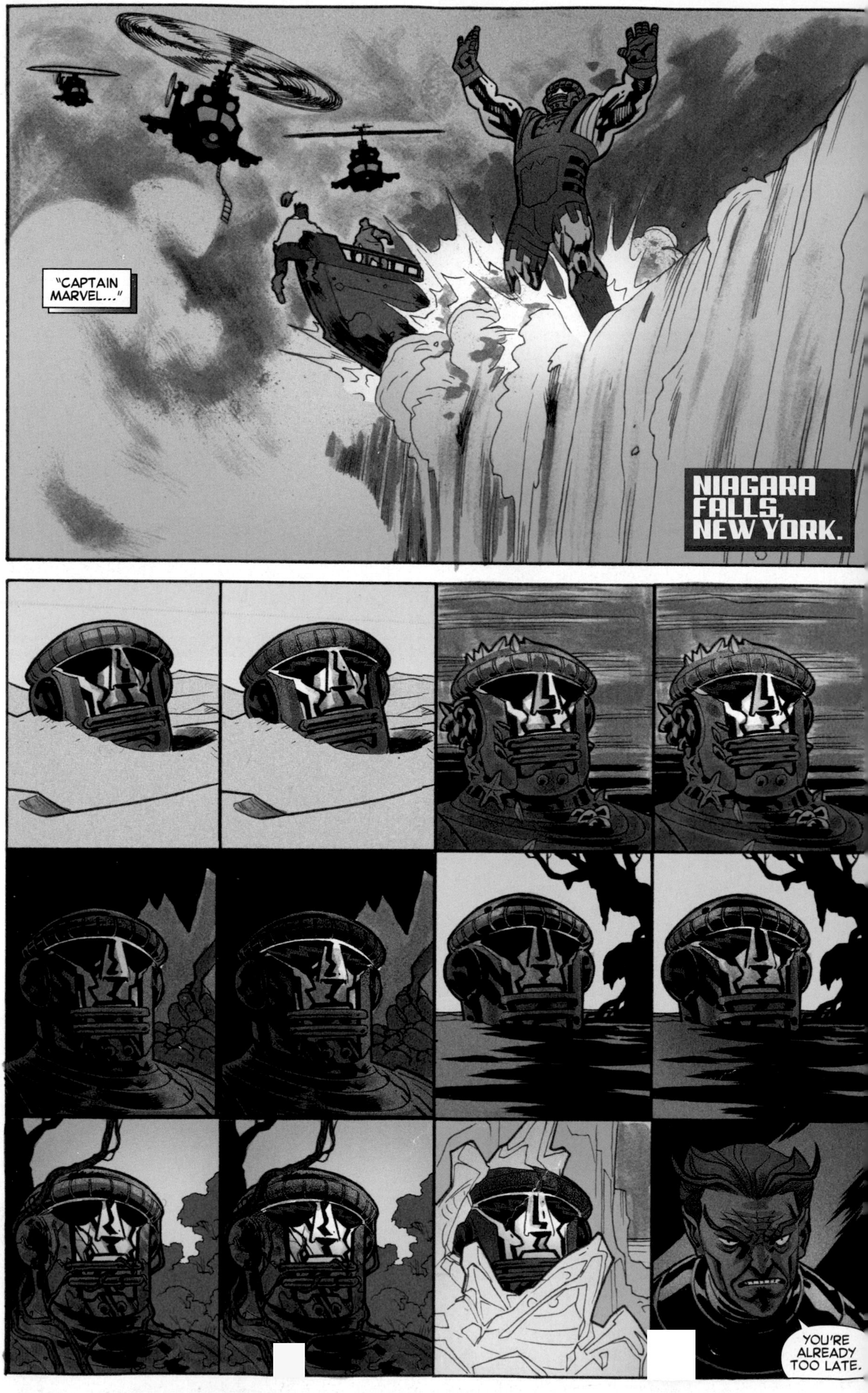
"CAPTAIN MARVEL..."
NIAGARA FALLS, NEW YORK.
YOU'RE ALREADY TOO LATE.

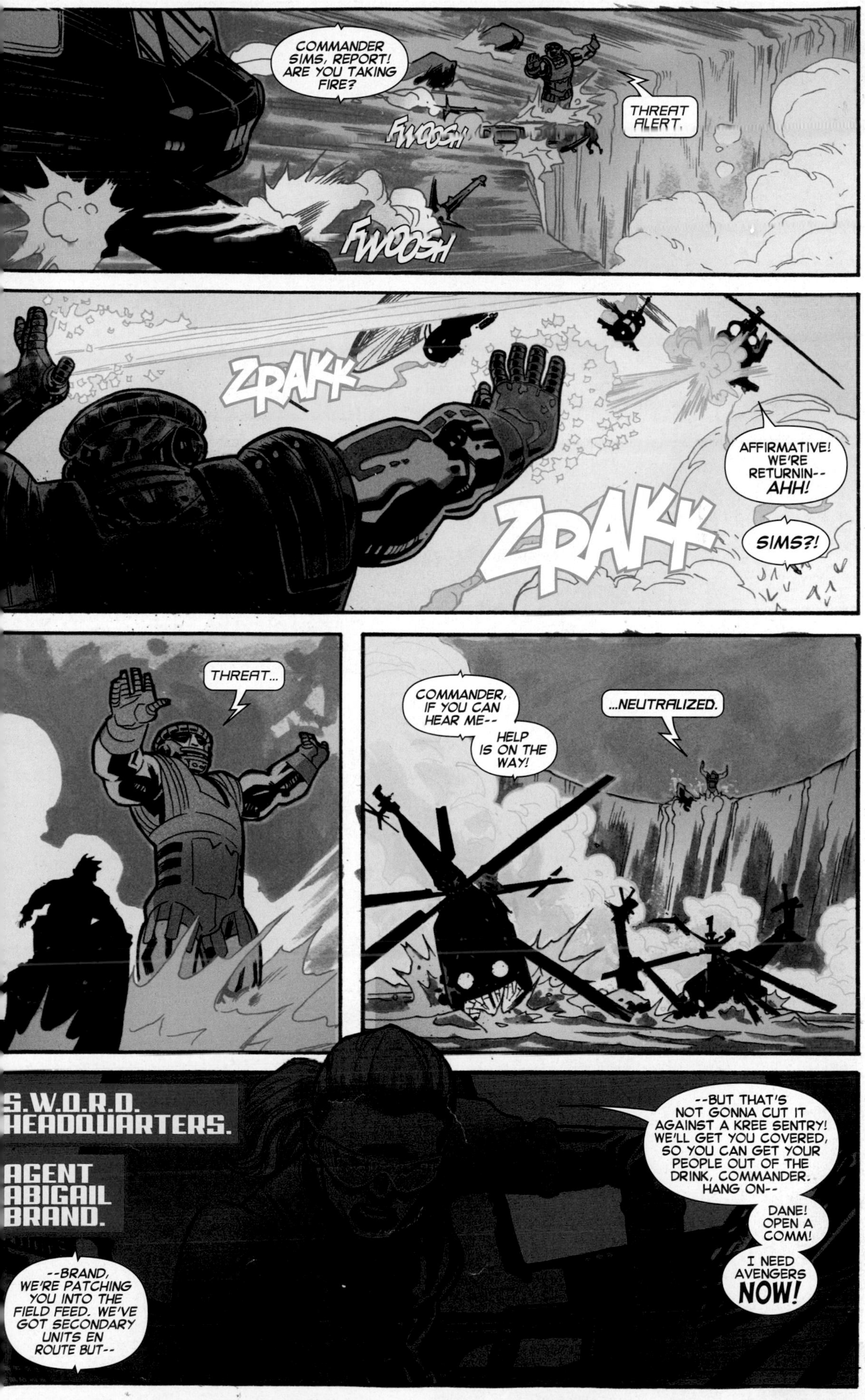
COMMANDER SIMS, REPORT! ARE YOU TAKING FIRE?
THREAT ALERT.
FWOOSH
FWOOSH
ZRAKK
AFFIRMATIVE! WE'RE RETURNIN-- AHH!
ZRAKK
SIMS?!
THREAT...
COMMANDER, IF YOU CAN HEAR ME--
HELP IS ON THE WAY!
...NEUTRALIZED.
S.W.O.R.D. HEADQUARTERS.
AGENT ABIGAIL BRAND.
--BRAND, WE'RE PATCHING YOU INTO THE FIELD FEED. WE'VE GOT SECONDARY UNITS EN ROUTE BUT--
--BUT THAT'S NOT GONNA CUT IT AGAINST A KREE SENTRY! WE'LL GET YOU COVERED, SO YOU CAN GET YOUR PEOPLE OUT OF THE DRINK, COMMANDER. HANG ON--
DANE! OPEN A COMM!
I NEED AVENGERS NOW!

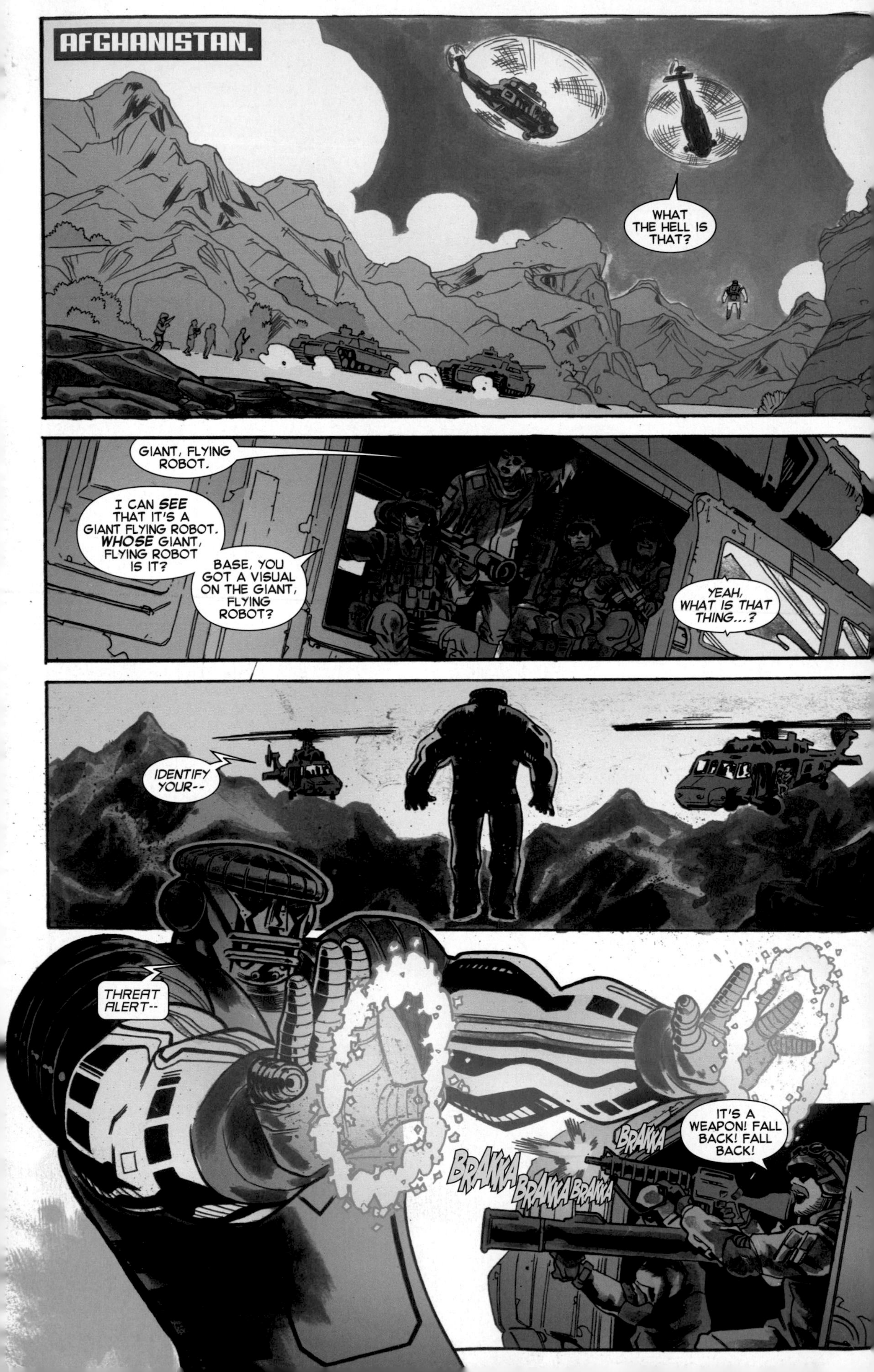
AFGHANISTAN.
WHAT THE HELL IS THAT?
GIANT, FLYING ROBOT.
I CAN SEE THAT IT'S A GIANT FLYING ROBOT. WHOSE GIANT, FLYING ROBOT IS IT?
BASE, YOU GOT A VISUAL ON THE GIANT, FLYING ROBOT?
YEAH, WHAT IS THAT THING...?
IDENTIFY YOUR--
THREAT ALERT--
IT'S A WEAPON! FALL BACK! FALL BACK!
BRAKKA
BRAKKA BRAKKA BRAKKA BRAKKA

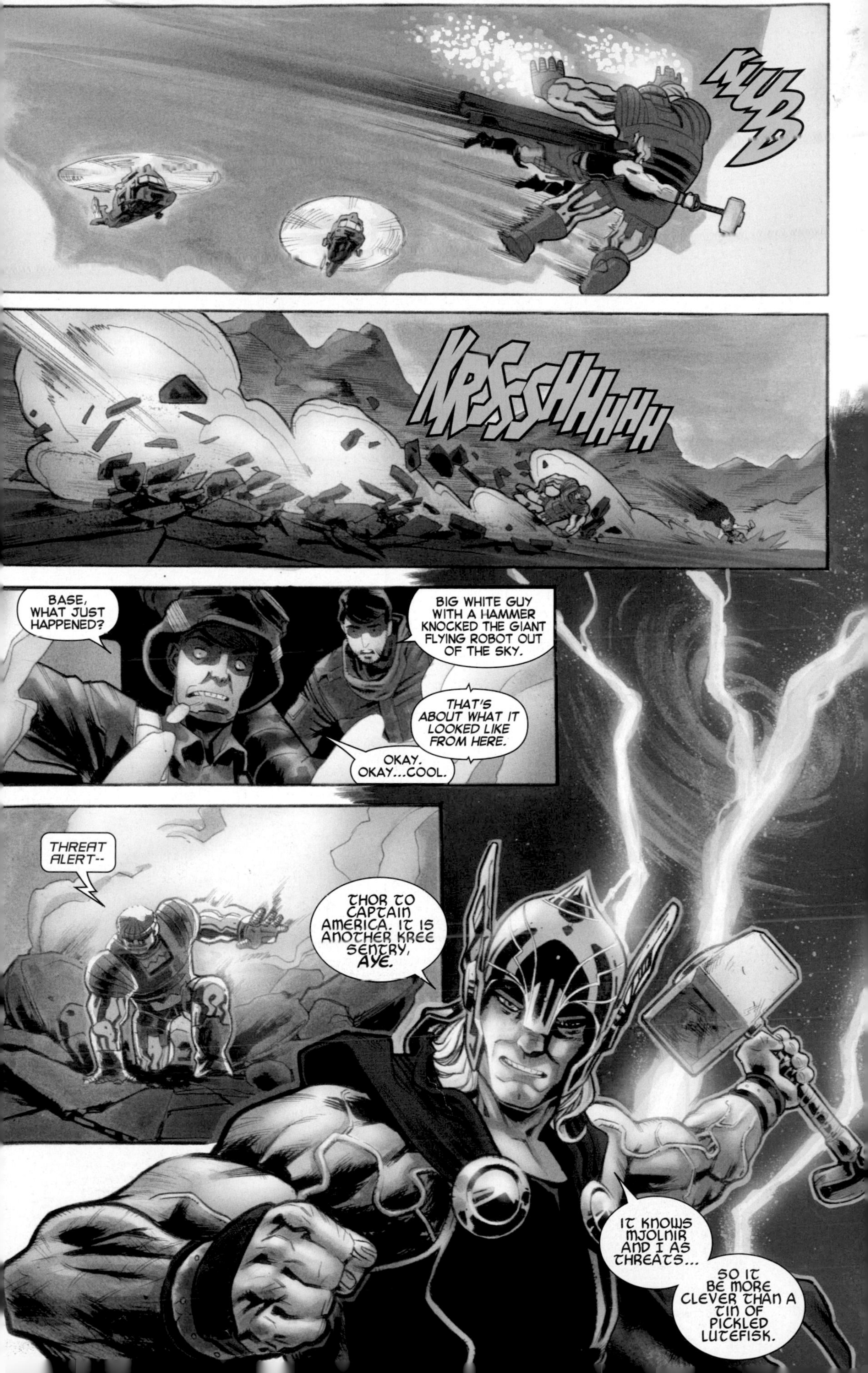
KUBB
KRSSSHHHHHH
BASE, WHAT JUST HAPPENED?
BIG WHITE GUY WITH A HAMMER KNOCKED THE GIANT FLYING ROBOT OUT OF THE SKY.
THAT'S ABOUT WHAT IT LOOKED LIKE FROM HERE.
OKAY. OKAY...COOL.
THREAT ALERT--
THOR TO CAPTAIN AMERICA. IT IS ANOTHER KREE SENTRY, AYE.
IT KNOWS MJOLNIR AND I AS THREATS...
SO IT BE MORE CLEVER THAN A TIN OF PICKLED LUTEFISK.

I'M TRYING TO BUILD AN ALGORITHM BUT I'M NOT FAST ENOUGH. MR. JARVIS, CAROL MENTIONED THAT MR. STARK SET SOMETHING UP SHE COULD TAP HER NETWORK INTO?

I DON'T NEED YOU TO COME! I UNDERSTAND THAT I CAN MONITOR AND COMMUNICATE FROM HERE, BUT THERE'S A REMOTE AUTHORIZATION REQUIRED AND I DON'T SEEM TO--

INDEED. I HADN'T PLANNED ON AN OUTING TODAY, BUT IF YOU LIKE I CAN COME BY MS. DANVER'S APARTMENT AND--

OH, OF COURSE, MS. KAWASAKI. ONE MOMENT.

ADJUNCT CONTROL CENTER PROTOCOL... RECOGNIZED.

PRIMARY SECURITY STRING... RECOGNIZED. JARVIS, EDWIN.

SECONDARY SECURITY STRING... RECOGNIZED. KAWASAKI, GWENDOLYN.

MS. KAWASAKI?

CENTER STATUS... ACTIVE.

YEAH... YEAH, I THINK THAT WAS IT.

OKAY, THANK YOU.

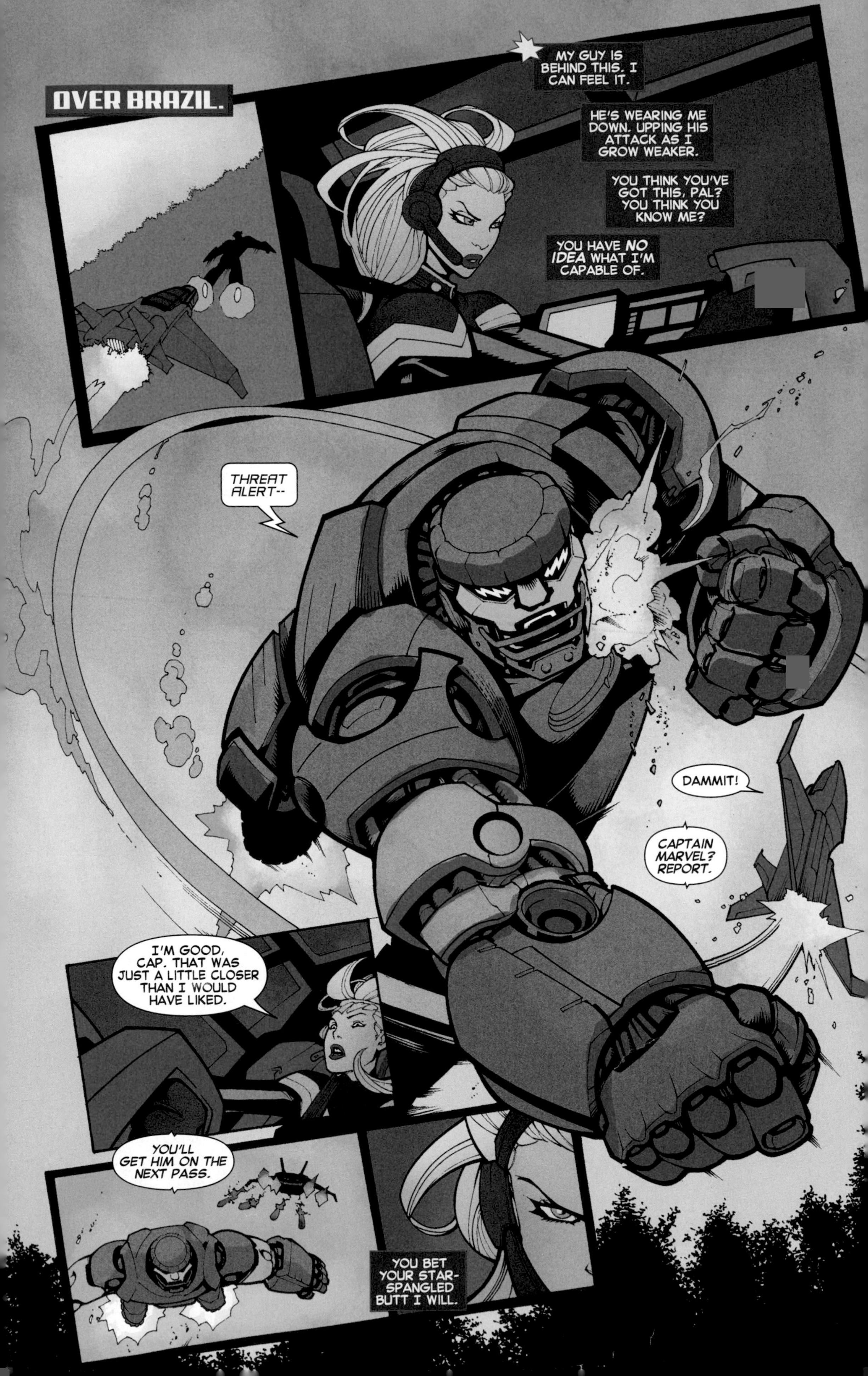
OVER BRAZIL.
MY GUY IS BEHIND THIS. I CAN FEEL IT.
HE'S WEARING ME DOWN. UPPING HIS ATTACK AS I GROW WEAKER.
YOU THINK YOU'VE GOT THIS, PAL? YOU THINK YOU KNOW ME?
YOU HAVE NO IDEA WHAT I'M CAPABLE OF.
THREAT ALERT--
DAMMIT!
CAPTAIN MARVEL? REPORT.
I'M GOOD, CAP. THAT WAS JUST A LITTLE CLOSER THAN I WOULD HAVE LIKED.
YOU'LL GET HIM ON THE NEXT PASS.
YOU BET YOUR STAR-SPANGLED BUTT I WILL.

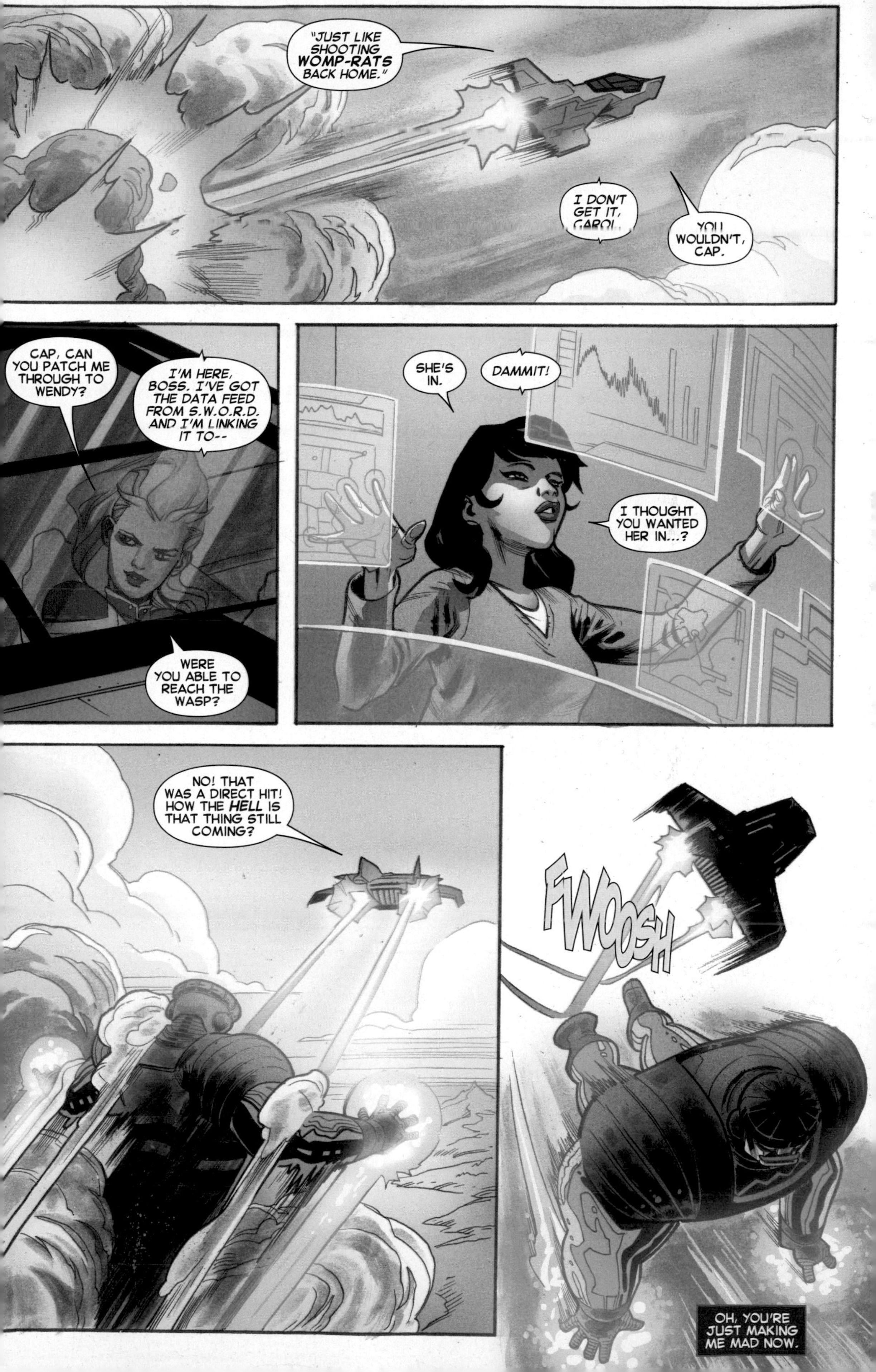
"JUST LIKE SHOOTING WOMP-RATS BACK HOME."
I DON'T GET IT, CAROL.
YOU WOULDN'T, CAP.
CAP, CAN YOU PATCH ME THROUGH TO WENDY?
I'M HERE, BOSS. I'VE GOT THE DATA FEED FROM S.W.O.R.D. AND I'M LINKING IT TO--
SHE'S IN.
DAMMIT!
I THOUGHT YOU WANTED HER IN...?
WERE YOU ABLE TO REACH THE WASP?
NO! THAT WAS A DIRECT HIT! HOW THE HELL IS THAT THING STILL COMING?
FWOOSH
OH, YOU'RE JUST MAKING ME MAD NOW.

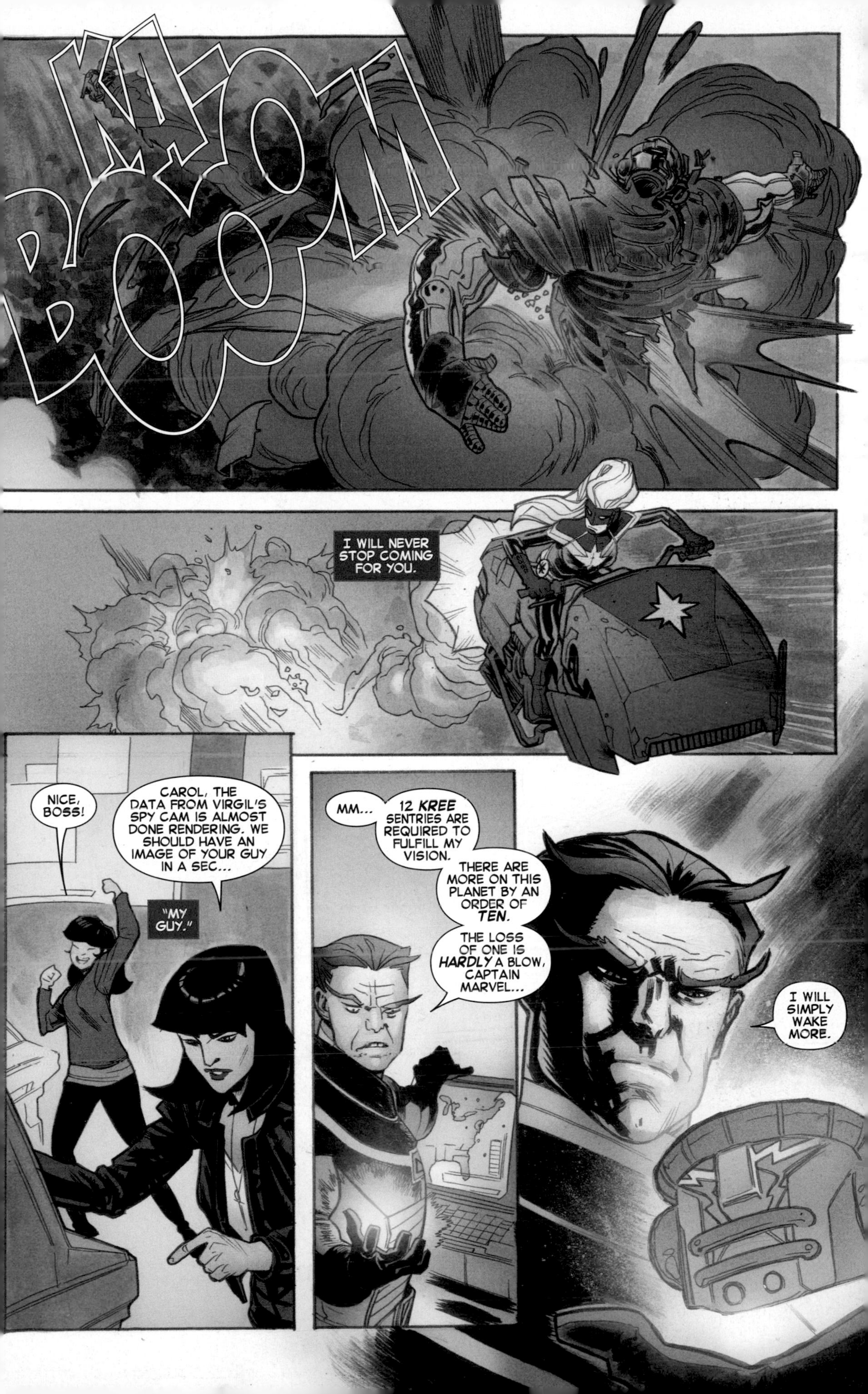
KA-BOOOM
I WILL NEVER STOP COMING FOR YOU.
NICE, BOSS!
CAROL, THE DATA FROM VIRGIL'S SPY CAM IS ALMOST DONE RENDERING. WE SHOULD HAVE AN IMAGE OF YOUR GUY IN A SEC...
"MY GUY."
MM...
12 KREE SENTRIES ARE REQUIRED TO FULFILL MY VISION.
THERE ARE MORE ON THIS PLANET BY AN ORDER OF TEN.
THE LOSS OF ONE IS HARDLY A BLOW, CAPTAIN MARVEL...
I WILL SIMPLY WAKE MORE.

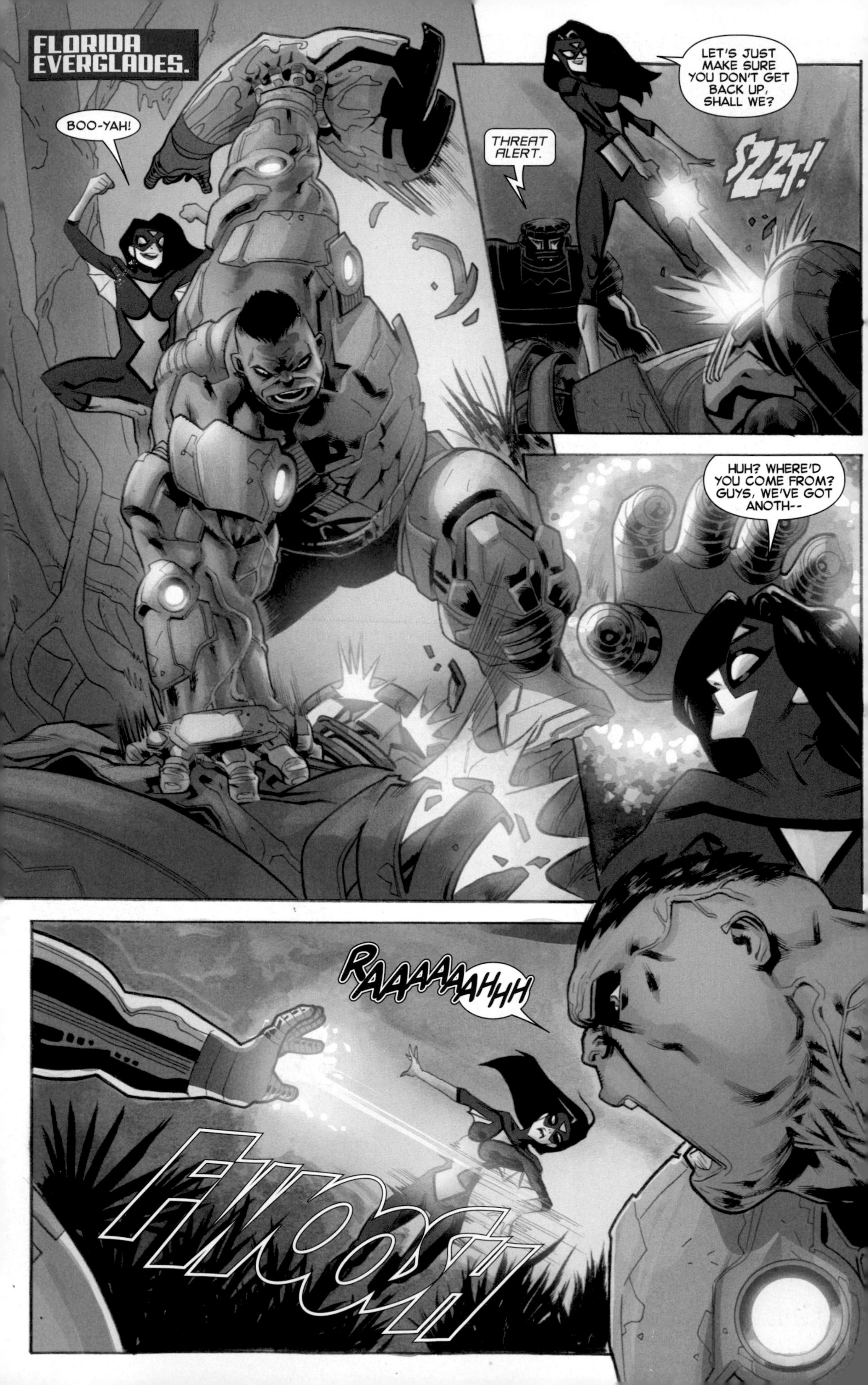
FLORIDA EVERGLADES.
BOO-YAH!
LET'S JUST MAKE SURE YOU DON'T GET BACK UP, SHALL WE?
THREAT ALERT.
SZZT!
HUH? WHERE'D YOU COME FROM? GUYS, WE'VE GOT ANOTH--
RAAAAAAHHH
FWOOSH

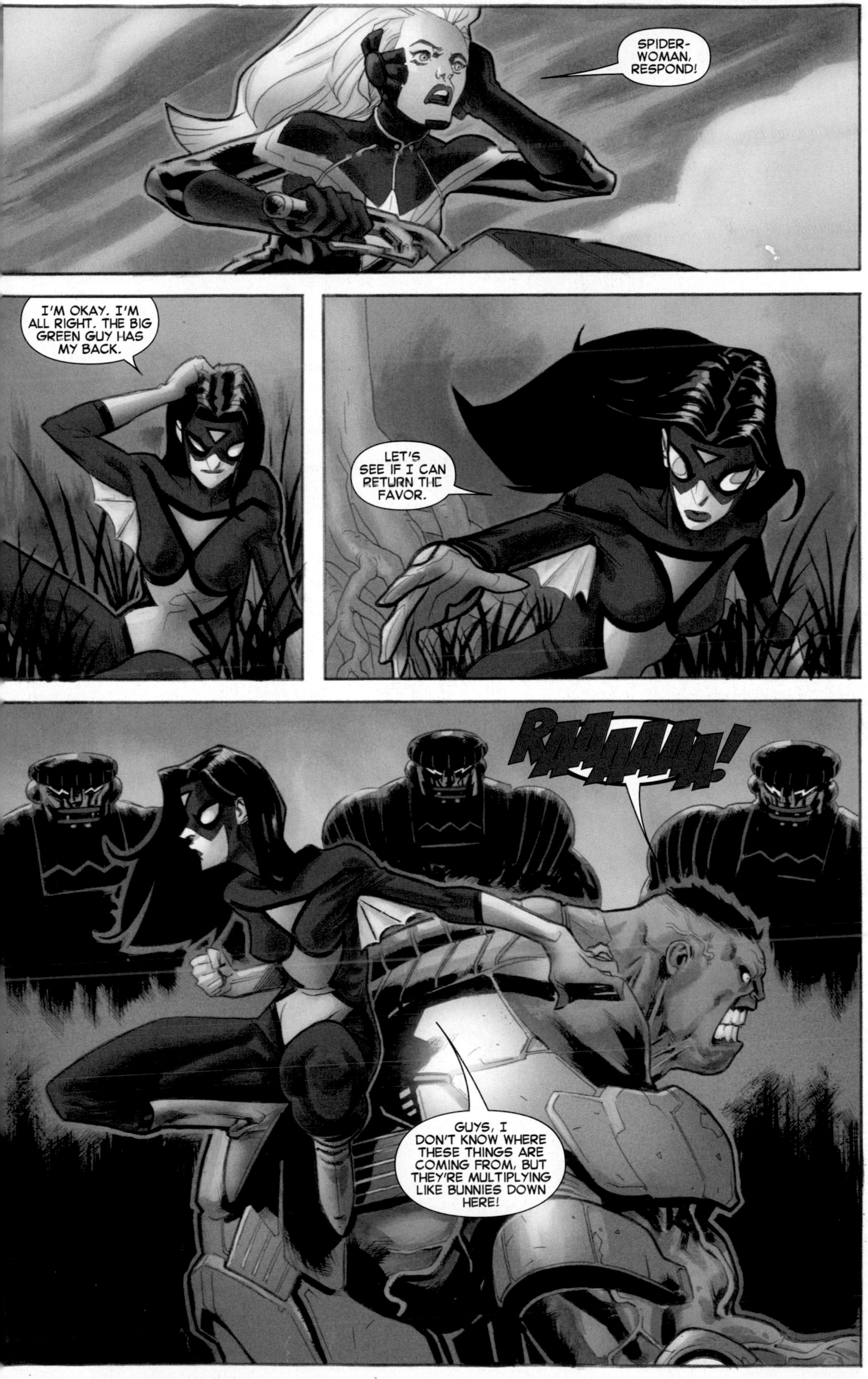
SPIDER-WOMAN, RESPOND!
I'M OKAY. I'M ALL RIGHT. THE BIG GREEN GUY HAS MY BACK.
LET'S SEE IF I CAN RETURN THE FAVOR.
GUYS, I DON'T KNOW WHERE THESE THINGS ARE COMING FROM, BUT THEY'RE MULTIPLYING LIKE BUNNIES DOWN HERE!

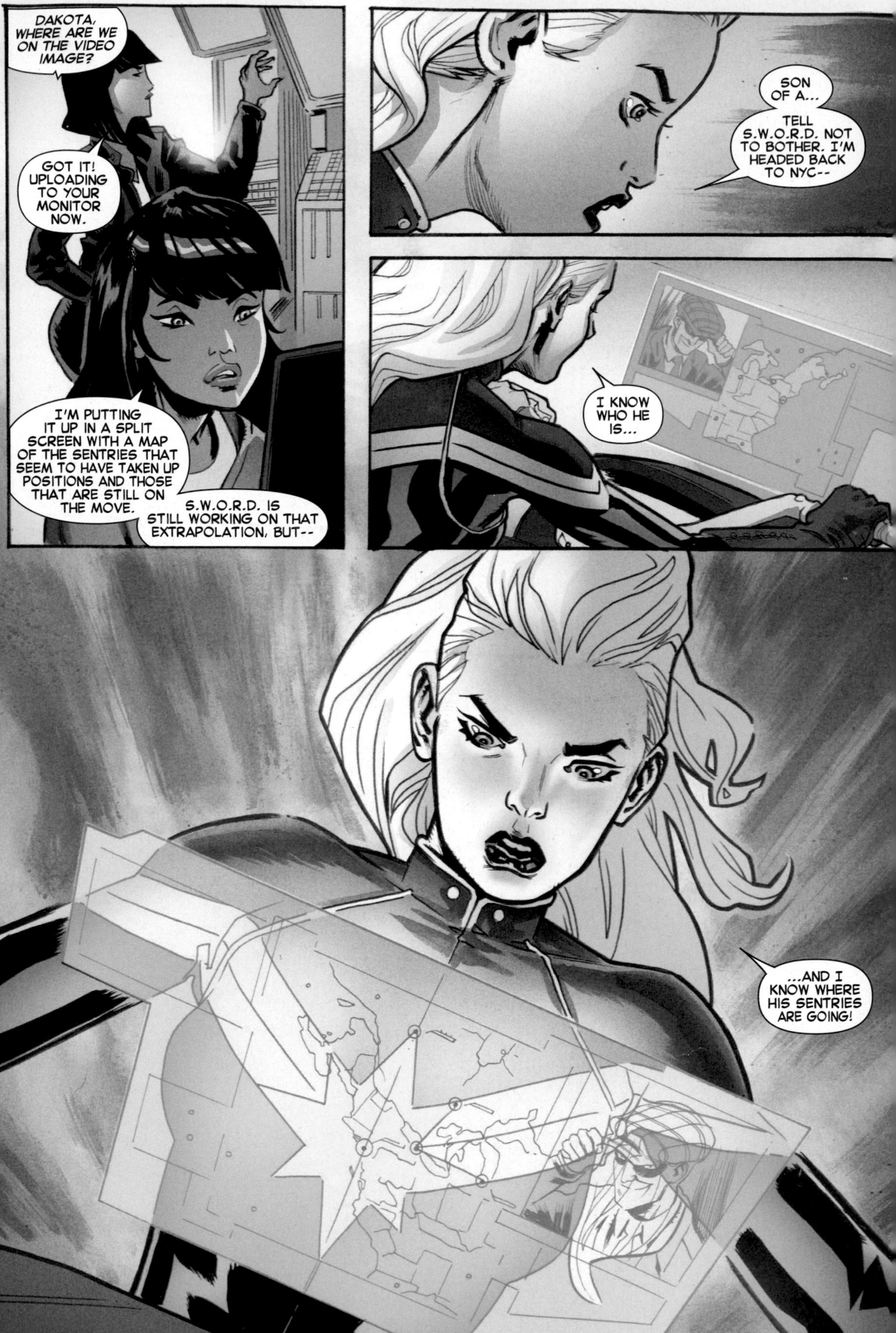
DAKOTA, WHERE ARE WE ON THE VIDEO IMAGE?
GOT IT! UPLOADING TO YOUR MONITOR NOW.
I'M PUTTING IT UP IN A SPLIT SCREEN WITH A MAP OF THE SENTRIES THAT SEEM TO HAVE TAKEN UP POSITIONS AND THOSE THAT ARE STILL ON THE MOVE.
S.W.O.R.D. IS STILL WORKING ON THAT EXTRAPOLATION, BUT--
SON OF A...
TELL S.W.O.R.D. NOT TO BOTHER. I'M HEADED BACK TO NYC--
I KNOW WHO HE IS...
...AND I KNOW WHERE HIS SENTRIES ARE GOING!

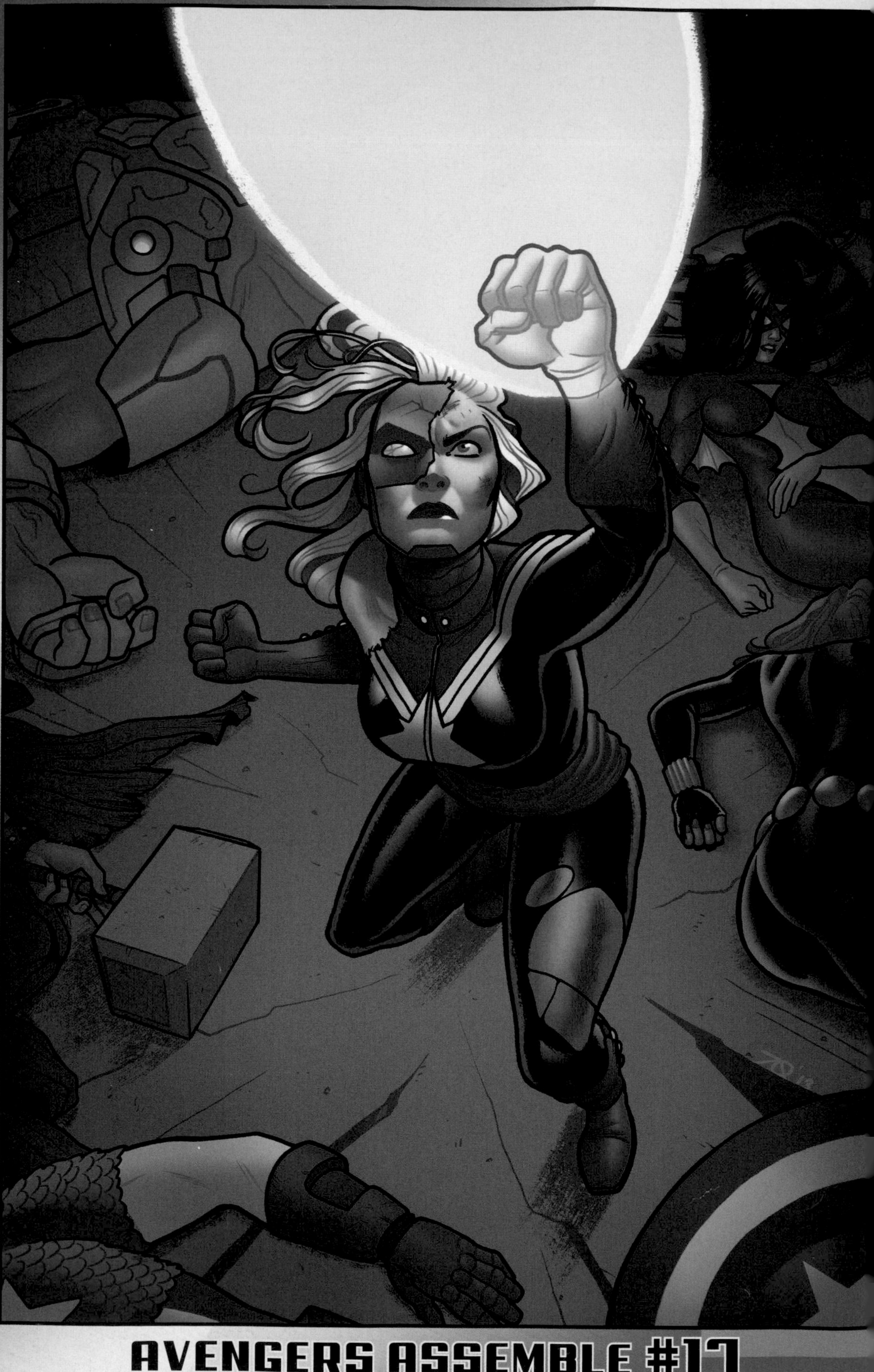

AVENGERS ASSEMBLE #17

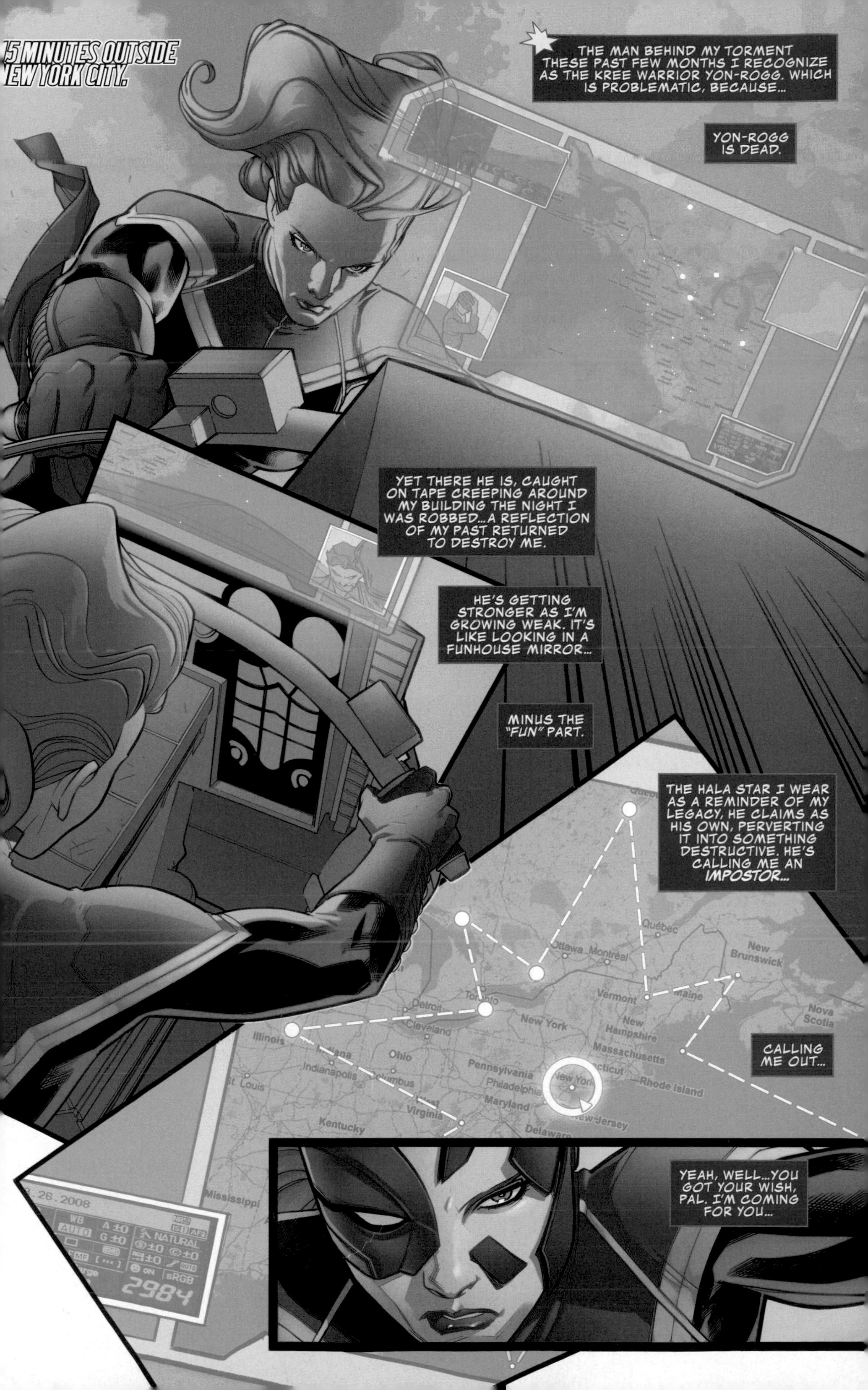
15 MINUTES OUTSIDE NEW YORK CITY.
THE MAN BEHIND MY TORMENT THESE PAST FEW MONTHS I RECOGNIZE AS THE KREE WARRIOR YON-ROGG. WHICH IS PROBLEMATIC, BECAUSE...
YON-ROGG IS DEAD.
YET THERE HE IS, CAUGHT ON TAPE CREEPING AROUND MY BUILDING THE NIGHT I WAS ROBBED...A REFLECTION OF MY PAST RETURNED TO DESTROY ME.
HE'S GETTING STRONGER AS I'M GROWING WEAK. IT'S LIKE LOOKING IN A FUNHOUSE MIRROR...
MINUS THE "FUN" PART.
THE HALA STAR I WEAR AS A REMINDER OF MY LEGACY, HE CLAIMS AS HIS OWN, PERVERTING IT INTO SOMETHING DESTRUCTIVE. HE'S CALLING ME AN *IMPOSTOR*...
CALLING ME OUT...
YEAH, WELL...YOU GOT YOUR WISH, PAL. I'M COMING FOR YOU...

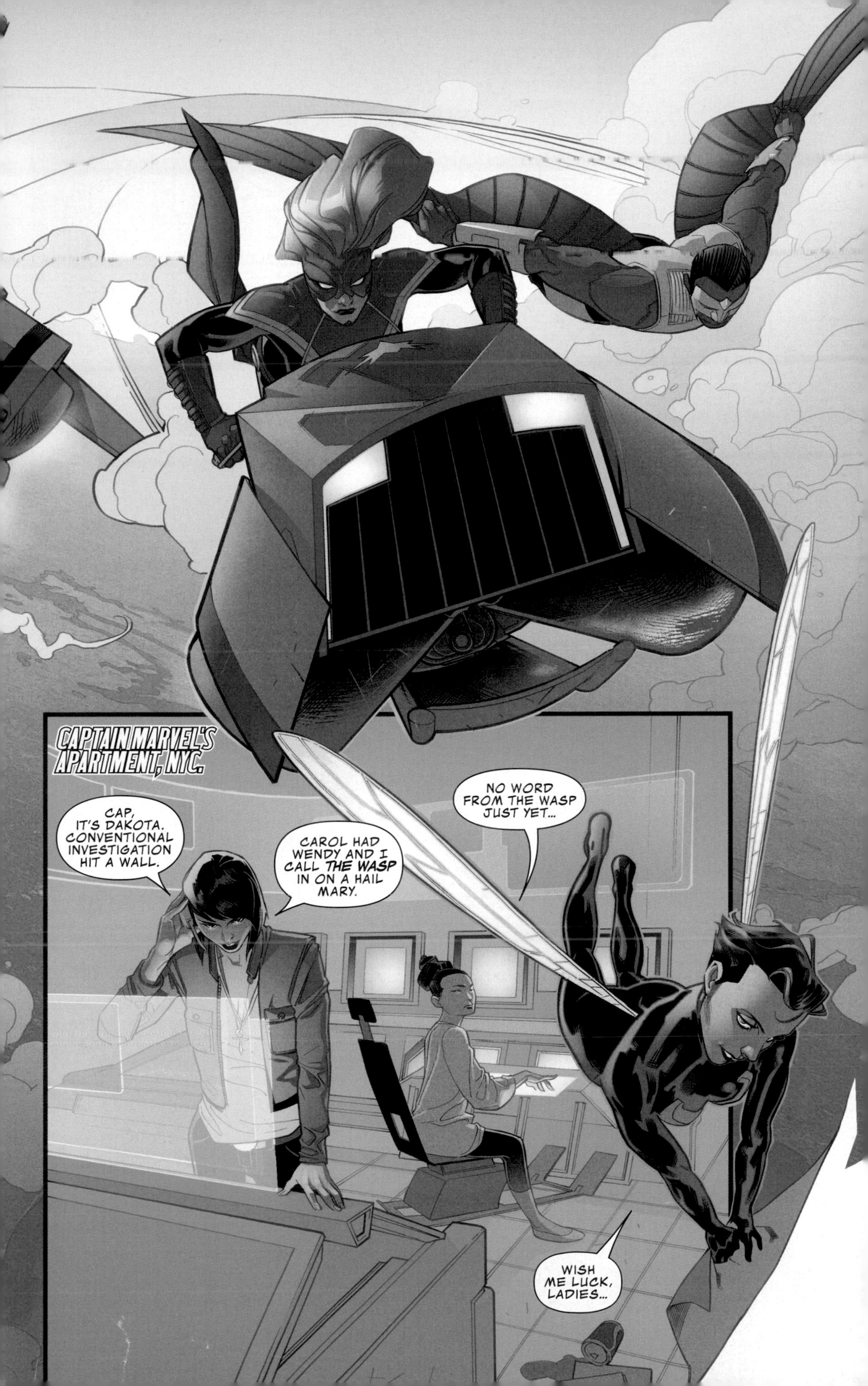
CAPTAIN MARVEL'S APARTMENT, NYC.
CAP, IT'S DAKOTA. CONVENTIONAL INVESTIGATION HIT A WALL.
CAROL HAD WENDY AND I CALL THE WASP IN ON A HAIL MARY.
NO WORD FROM THE WASP JUST YET...
WISH ME LUCK, LADIES...

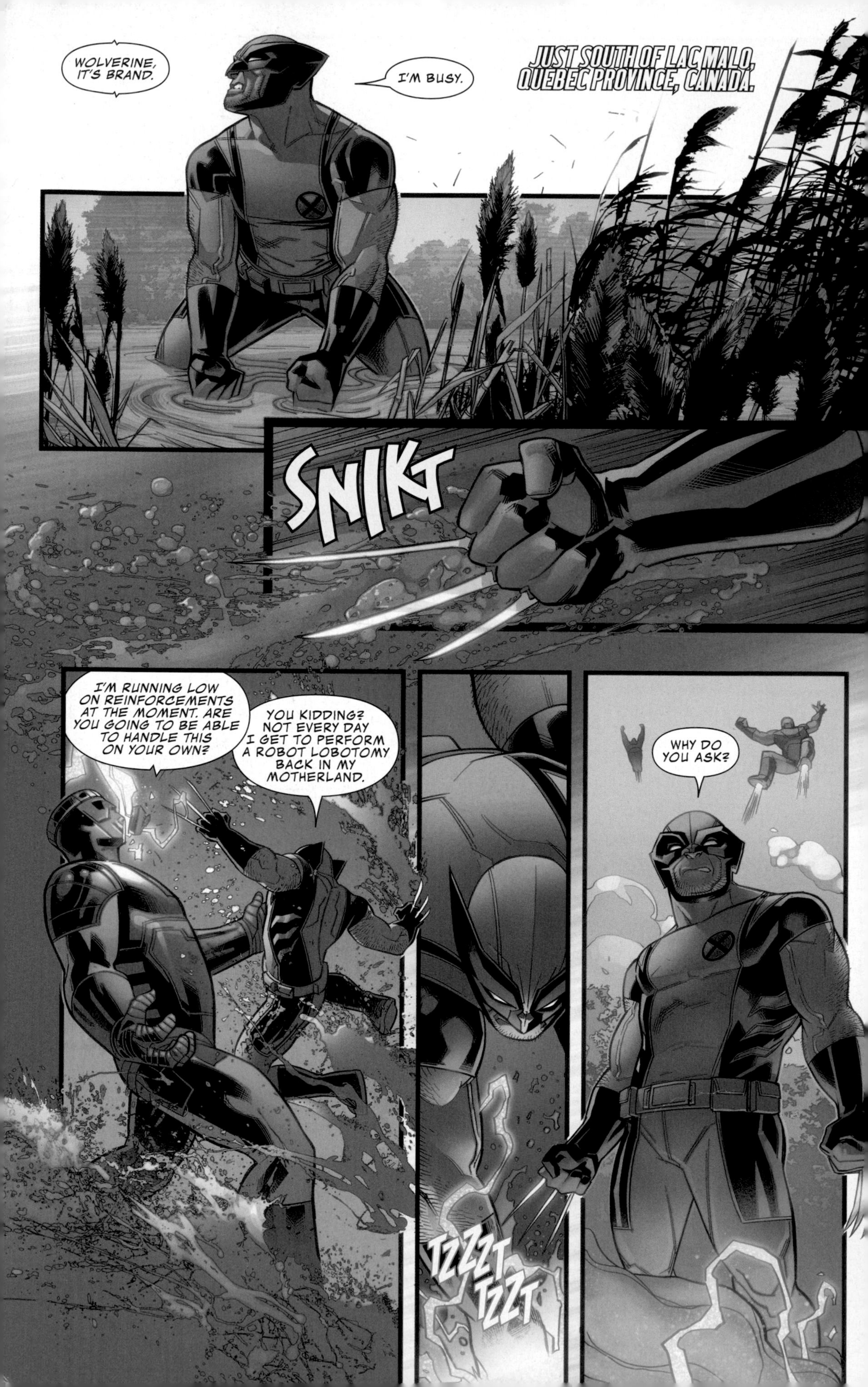
WOLVERINE, IT'S BRAND.
I'M BUSY.
JUST SOUTH OF LAC MALO, QUEBEC PROVINCE, CANADA.
SNIKT
I'M RUNNING LOW ON REINFORCEMENTS AT THE MOMENT. ARE YOU GOING TO BE ABLE TO HANDLE THIS ON YOUR OWN?
YOU KIDDING? NOT EVERY DAY I GET TO PERFORM A ROBOT LOBOTOMY BACK IN MY MOTHERLAND.
TZZZT TZZT
WHY DO YOU ASK?

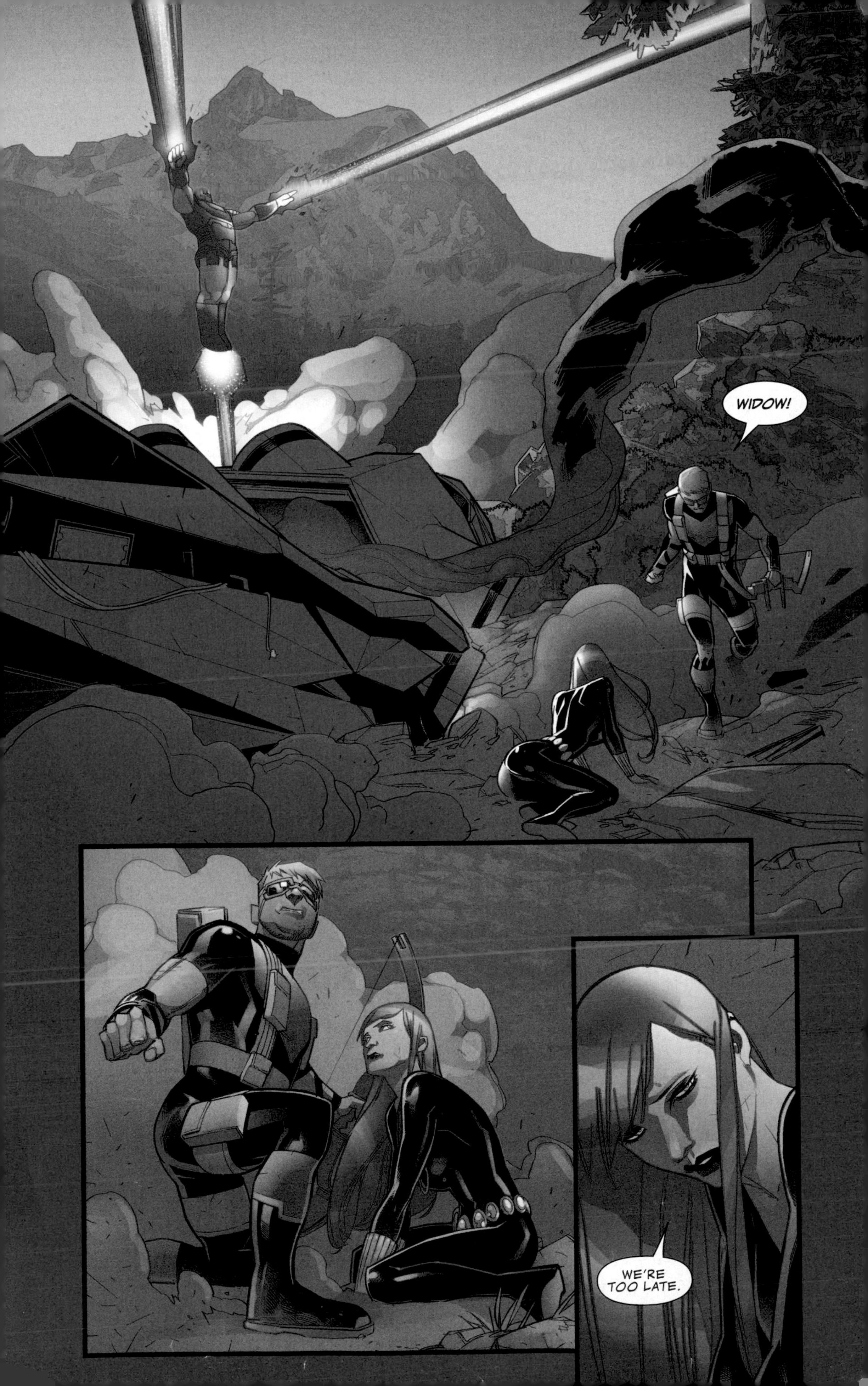
WIDOW!
WE'RE TOO LATE.

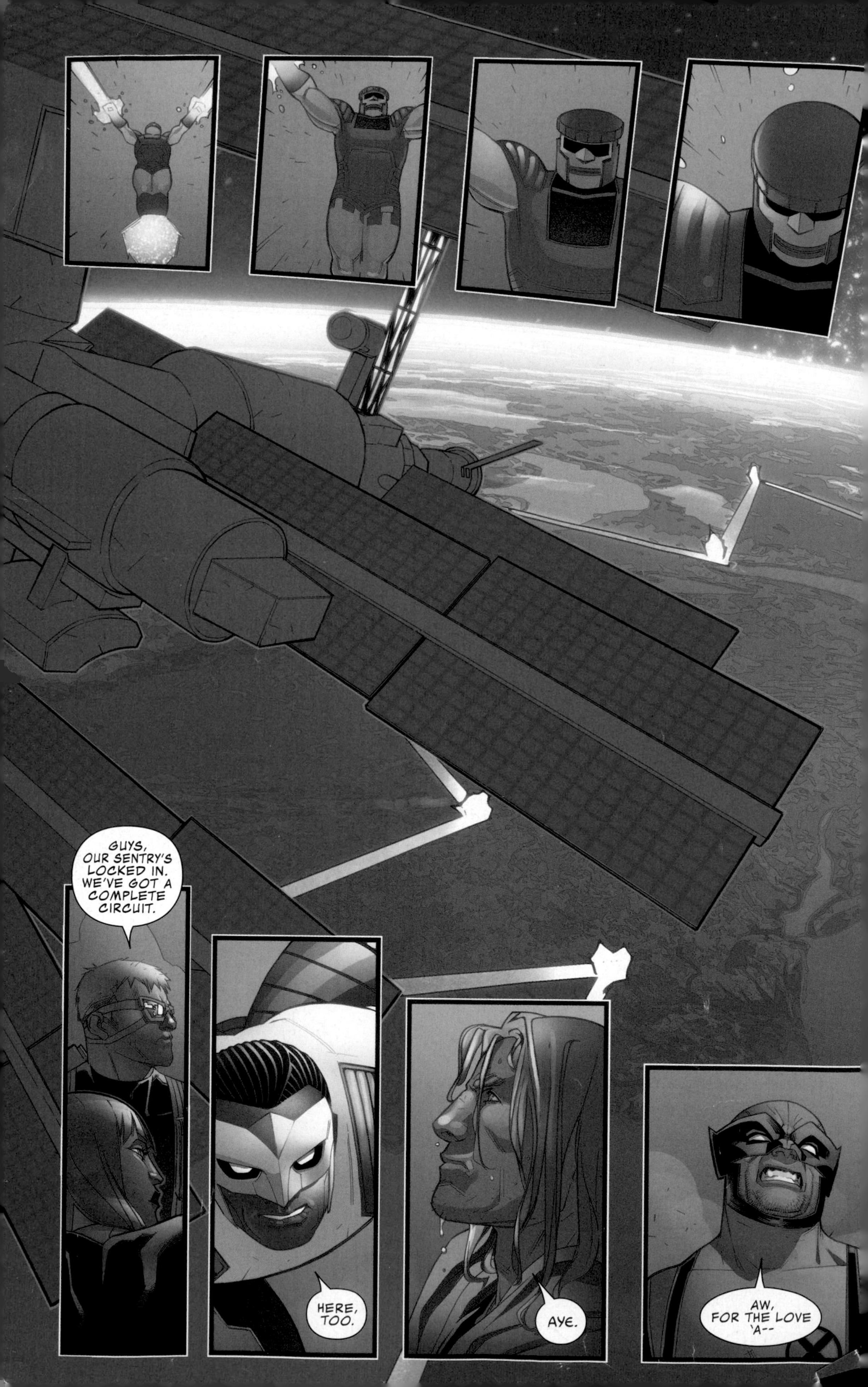
GUYS, OUR SENTRY'S LOCKED IN. WE'VE GOT A COMPLETE CIRCUIT.
HERE, TOO.
AYE.
AW, FOR THE LOVE 'A--

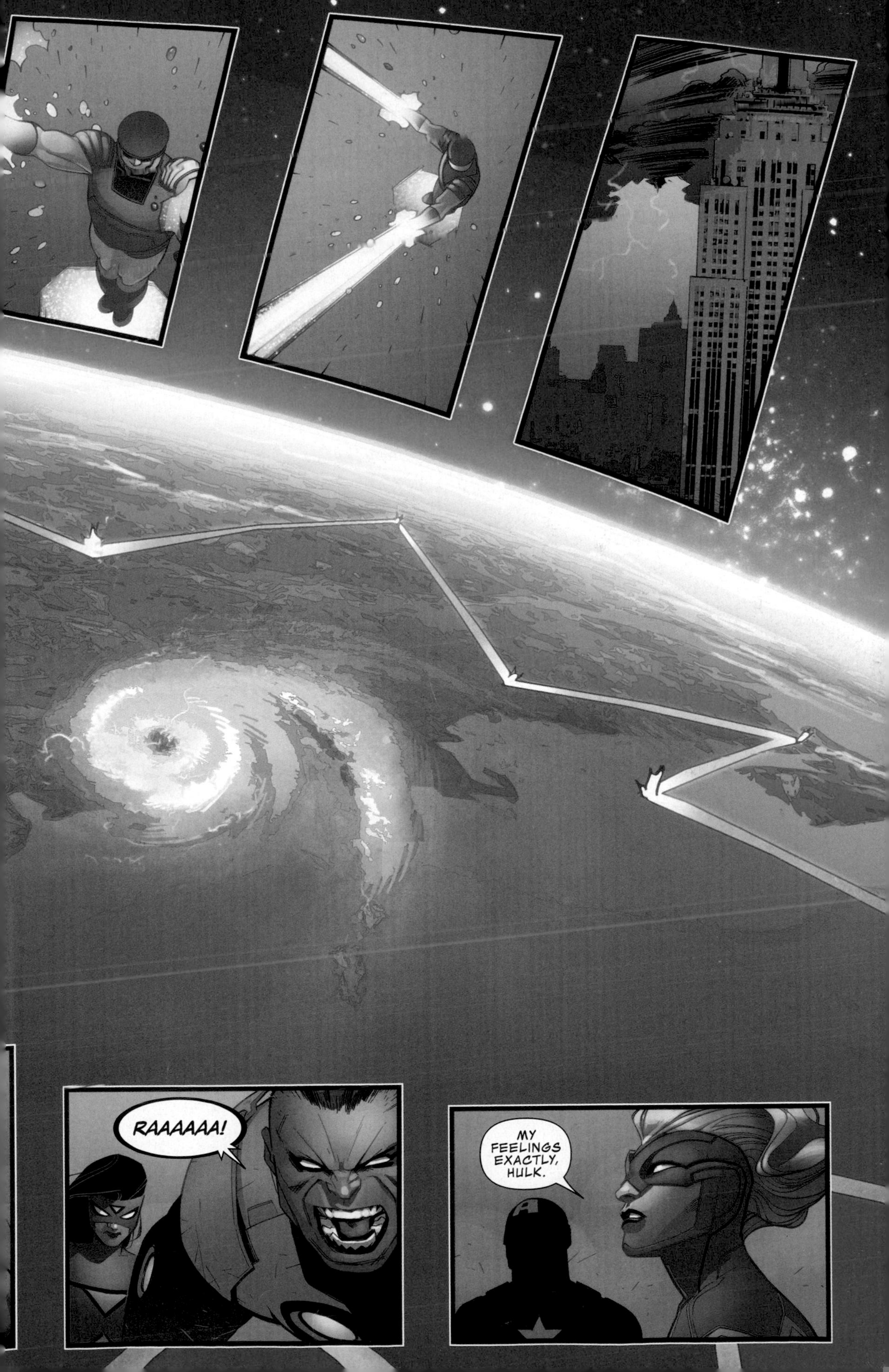
RAAAAAA!
MY FEELINGS EXACTLY, HULK.

ATTENTION, S.W.O.R.D.! I WANT TO KNOW WHAT THE HELL IS FORMING OVER NEW YORK CITY AND WHERE THE HELL IT CAME FROM.

I WANT A SCAN OF A THREE BLOCK RADIUS AROUND 54TH AND LEX, AND IF THERE ARE ANY HOSTILE SIGNATURES AT ALL, I WANT THEIR EXACT COORDINATES.

AGENT BRAND, I'VE GOT PROJECT P.E.G.A.S.U.S. ON THE LINE.

I DON'T HAVE TIME FOR P.E.G.A.S.U.S. PROBLEMS TODAY.

SIR, THE CAPTURED BROOD HAVE DISAPPEARED.

THEY'RE NO LONGER IN P.E.G.A.S.U.S. CUSTODY.

ON TOP OF EVERYTHING ELSE, I'VE GOT BROOD ON THE LOOSE?

NO, SIR. THEY DISAPPEARED AS IN, WEN' POOF.

SAME WITH THE DINOSAURS SIR. THE DINOSAURS.

RRRRAAGH!

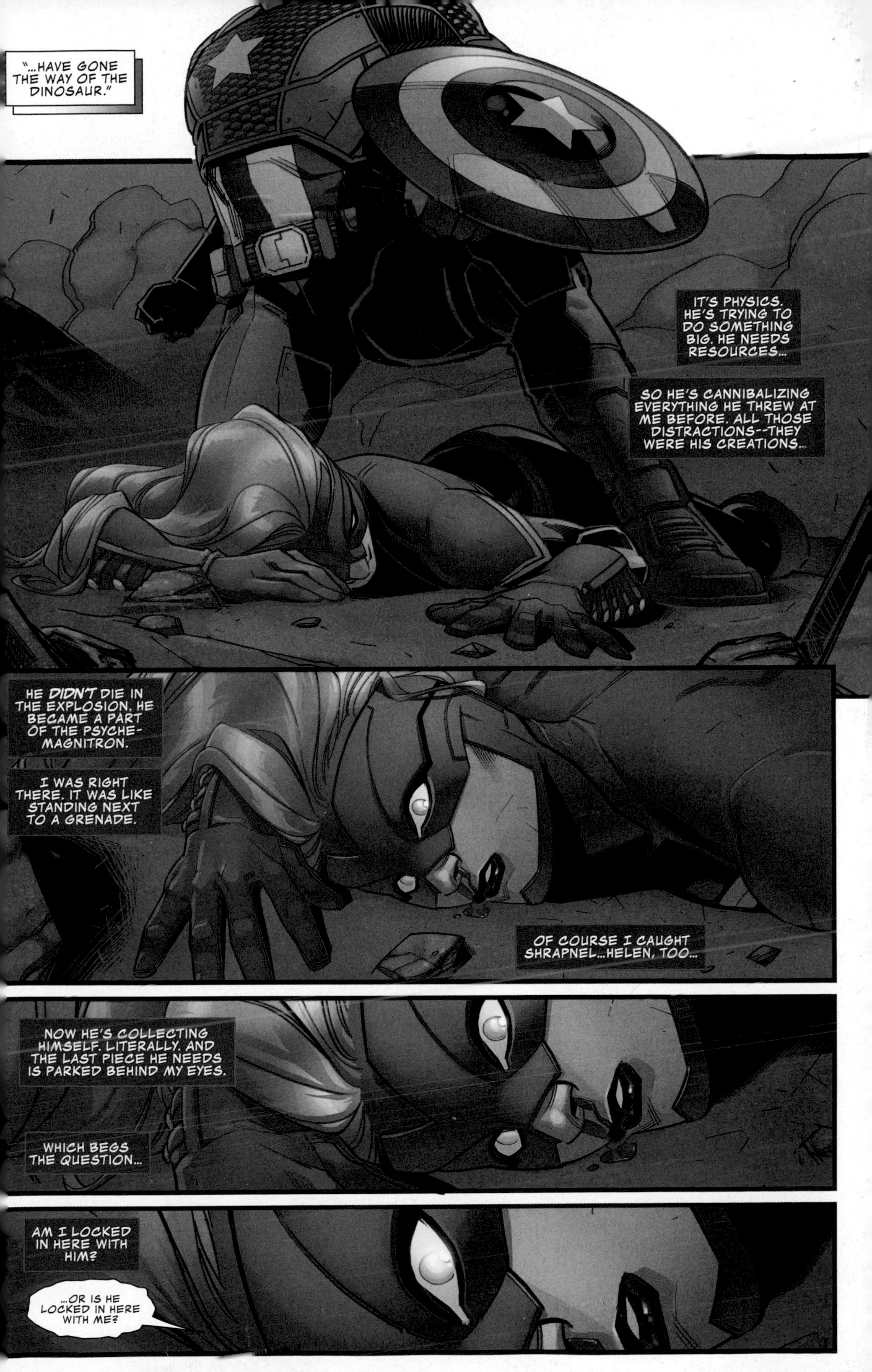
"...HAVE GONE THE WAY OF THE DINOSAUR."
IT'S PHYSICS. HE'S TRYING TO DO SOMETHING BIG. HE NEEDS RESOURCES...
SO HE'S CANNIBALIZING EVERYTHING HE THREW AT ME BEFORE. ALL THOSE DISTRACTIONS--THEY WERE HIS CREATIONS...
HE DIDN'T DIE IN THE EXPLOSION. HE BECAME A PART OF THE PSYCHE-MAGNITRON.
I WAS RIGHT THERE. IT WAS LIKE STANDING NEXT TO A GRENADE.
OF COURSE I CAUGHT SHRAPNEL...HELEN, TOO...
NOW HE'S COLLECTING HIMSELF. LITERALLY. AND THE LAST PIECE HE NEEDS IS PARKED BEHIND MY EYES.
WHICH BEGS THE QUESTION...
AM I LOCKED IN HERE WITH HIM?
...OR IS HE LOCKED IN HERE WITH ME?

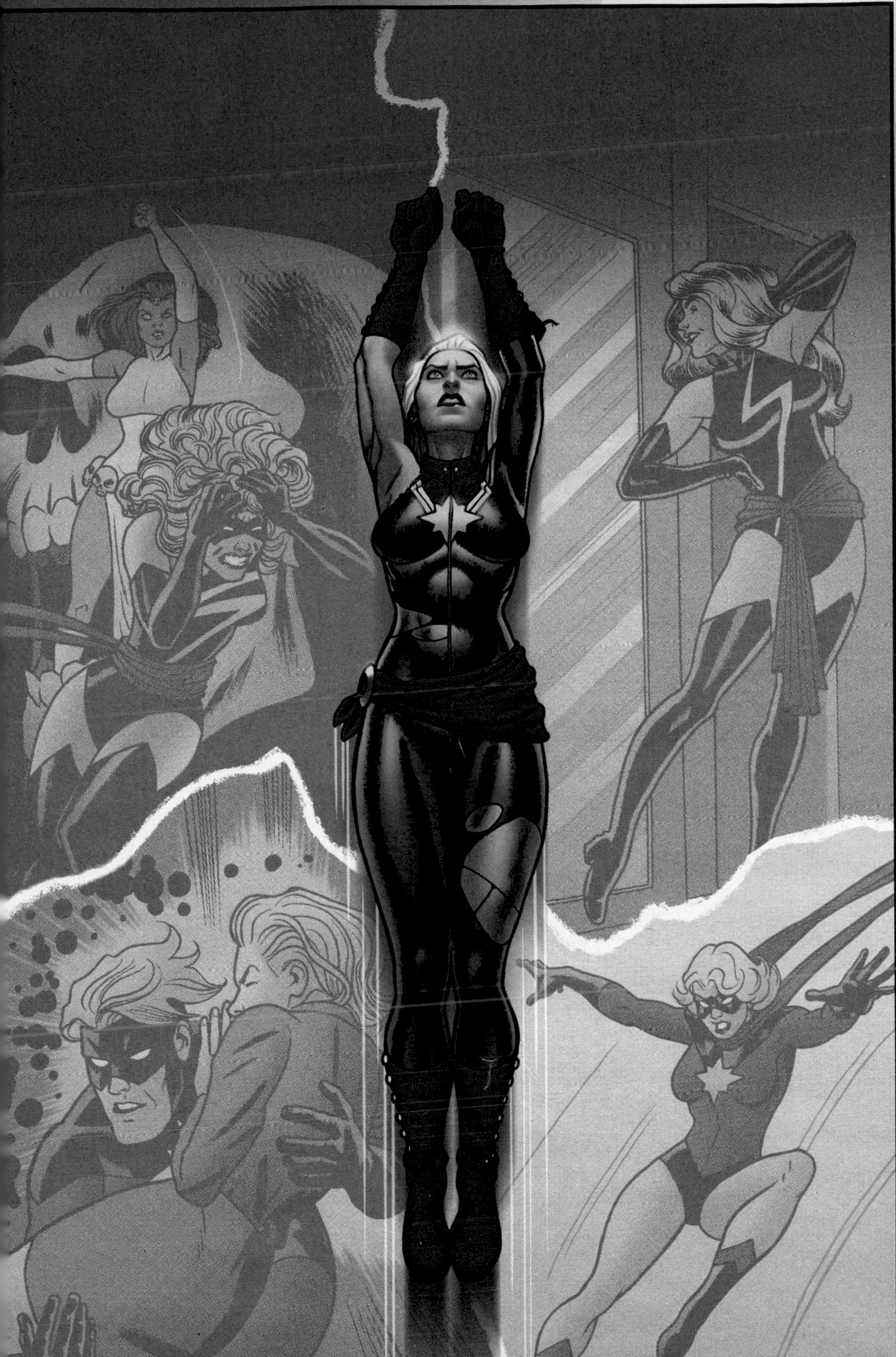

CAPTAIN MARVEL #14

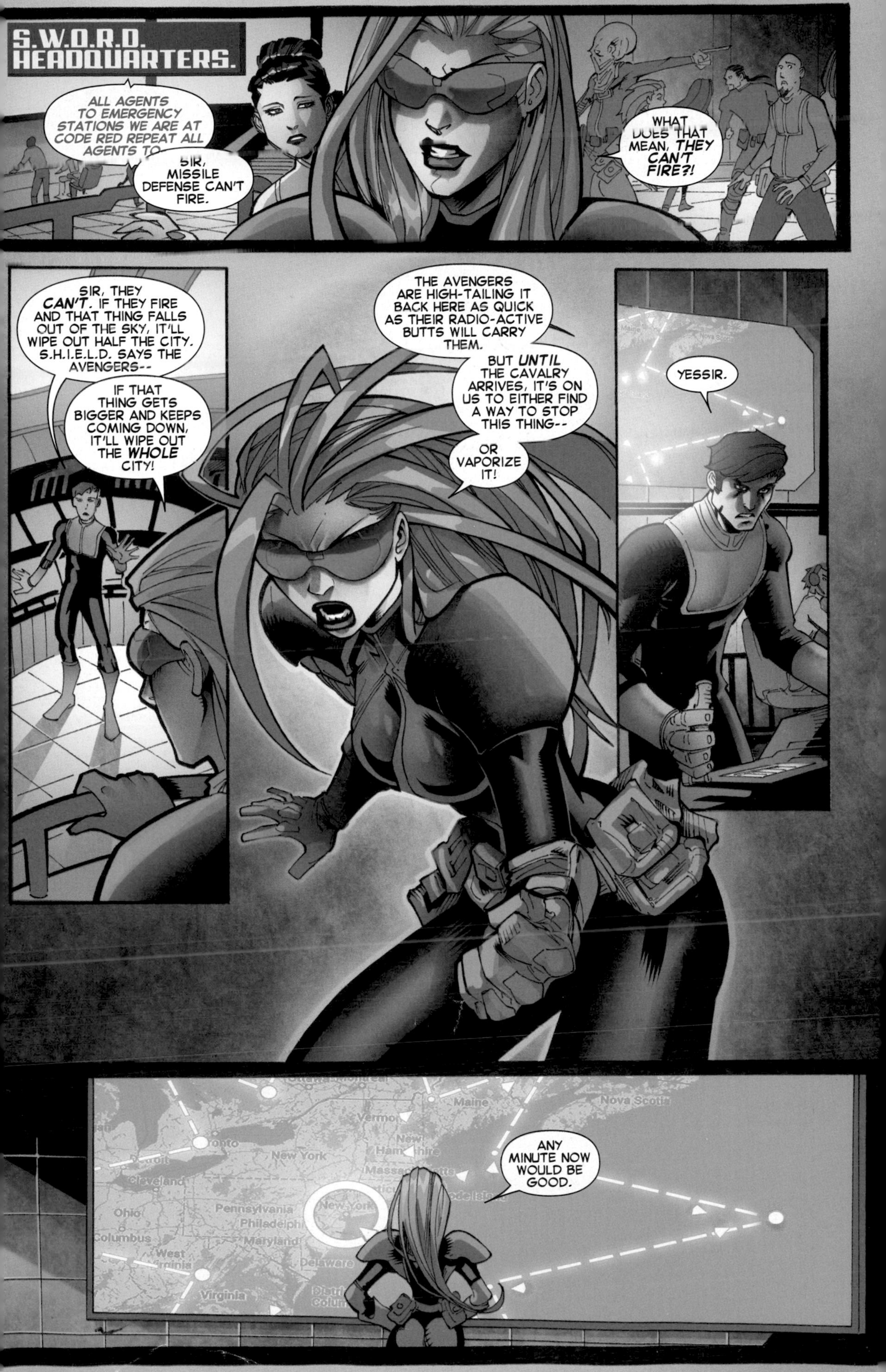
S.W.O.R.D. HEADQUARTERS.
ALL AGENTS TO EMERGENCY STATIONS WE ARE AT CODE RED REPEAT ALL AGENTS TO
SIR, MISSILE DEFENSE CAN'T FIRE.
WHAT DOES THAT MEAN, THEY CAN'T FIRE?!
SIR, THEY CAN'T. IF THEY FIRE AND THAT THING FALLS OUT OF THE SKY, IT'LL WIPE OUT HALF THE CITY. S.H.I.E.L.D. SAYS THE AVENGERS--
IF THAT THING GETS BIGGER AND KEEPS COMING DOWN, IT'LL WIPE OUT THE WHOLE CITY!
THE AVENGERS ARE HIGH-TAILING IT BACK HERE AS QUICK AS THEIR RADIO-ACTIVE BUTTS WILL CARRY THEM.
BUT UNTIL THE CAVALRY ARRIVES, IT'S ON US TO EITHER FIND A WAY TO STOP THIS THING--
OR VAPORIZE IT!
YESSIR.
Maine
Nova Scotia
New York
Cleveland
Ohio
Pennsylvania
Philadelphia
Maryland
Columbus
West Virginia
Virginia
Delaware
ANY MINUTE NOW WOULD BE GOOD.

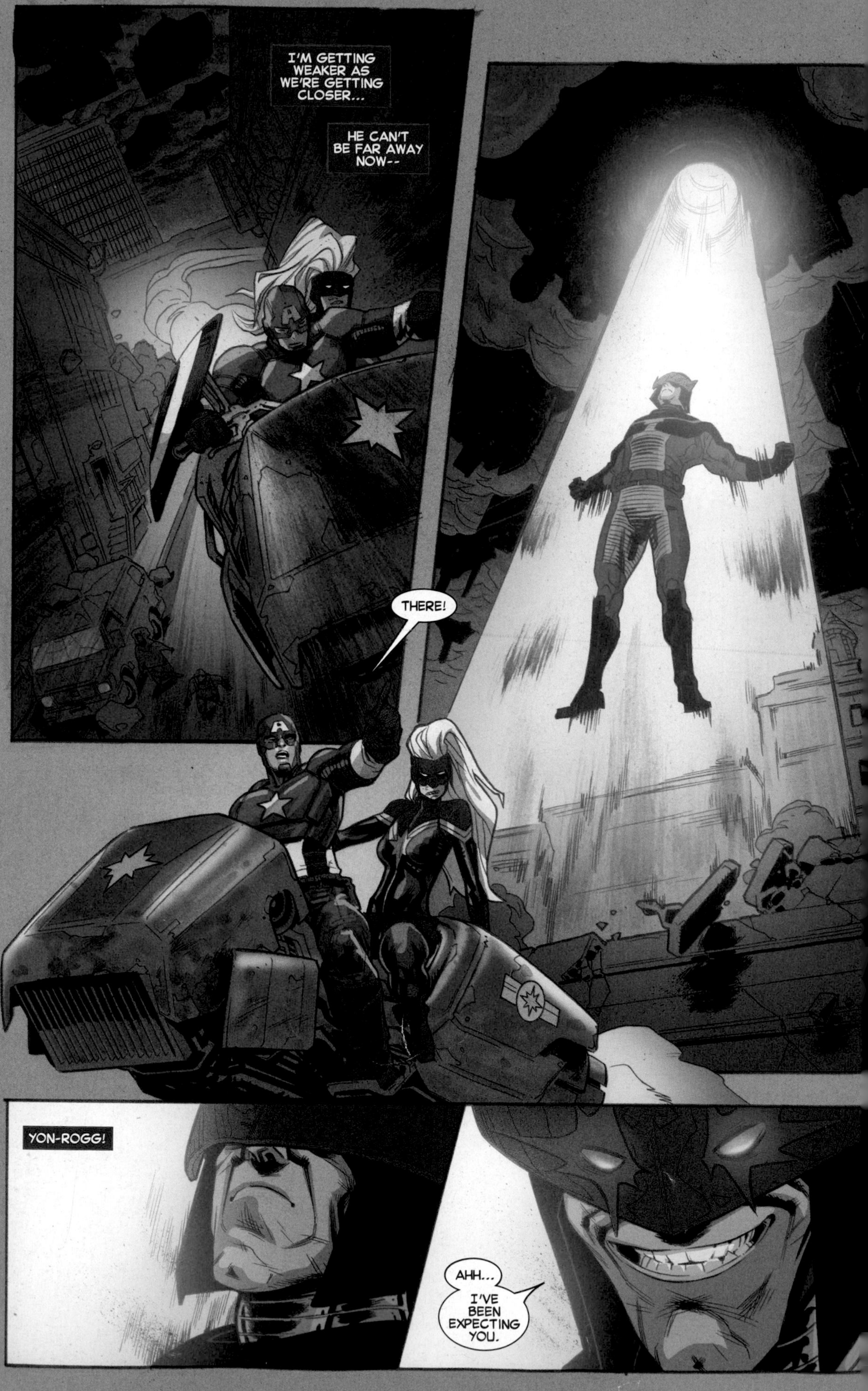
I'M GETTING WEAKER AS WE'RE GETTING CLOSER...
HE CAN'T BE FAR AWAY NOW--
THERE!
YON-ROGG!
AHH...
I'VE BEEN EXPECTING YOU.

LET'S RAP WITH CAP

SANA AMANAT
EDITOR

STEPHEN WACKER
SENIOR EDITOR

AXEL ALONSO
EDITOR-IN-CHIEF

JOE QUESADA
CHIEF CREATIVE OFFICE

DAN BUCKLEY
PUBLISHER

ALAN FINE
EXECUTIVE PRODUCER

Send letters to:
mheroes@marvel.com • 135 W 50TH ST, 7TH FLOOR, NEW YORK, NY 10020 (PLEASE MARK OKAY TO PRINT)

Didn't think we'd end it like that, did ya? Don't worry we did NOT kill Captain Marvel. If you missed the previews, Carol's about to jump into an Infinity adventure next month. However, she will be slightly different the next time you see her. That's all I'm sharing for now—even if you try to bribe me with cookies or chocolate covered strawberries or something—I'll never tell! But I mean, no harm in *trying* (strawberries are in season, bt-dubs).

I think that Carol's strength as a hero has little to do with her actual powers and more to do with what she chooses to do with them— protect those she loves. As her little protégé Kit stood by and watched her beloved champion beat the bad guy once again, I started wondering what it actually meant to be someone's hero. Recently, my niece Zayna made my heart melt when she named me her hero for a school project and presented me with this swanky award:

Usually this is where I'd turn into a braggart, but I was honestly so touched by the gesture—and confused as to why she picked me— that I was tearing throughout the ceremony. It dawned on me then that I actually have a lot of responsibility on my hands to *not screw it all up!* I have a nine-year-old niece who actually thinks I'm worthy--so now I've got to live up to that image and make sure that everything I do is a positive example for her. Until, of course, she's old enough to realize I'm a farce! (Kidding, ZZ, thanks for picking me, I love you!)

We've all got our heroes in the real world. Whether they're people who actually save lives, or people who teach you how to ride a bike— they're the ones who make you want to be a better person, too. So in the effort to honor our real life heroes, I asked the rest of the Captain Marvel team who they'd name as theirs...

I've been blessed with so many. On my mind right now, my great aunt who we call "Gamma Polly." Heroes are defined by their courage and nobility. I could spend all day telling you stories of Polly's noble acts, but it's her courage in the face of her cancer struggle that moves me to name her. She's modeling a kind of grace and compassion that doesn't just put me in awe of her, but of what we as human beings are capable of.

–Kelly Sue DeConnick

My dearest personal hero is my Dad for his constant selfless acts of kindness.

–Jordie Bellaire

I'm inspired by teachers who wake up every morning and prepare my kids for the future. With little pay and no fame, they are some of the most important people in our society.

–Steve Wacker

Jim Troy, my dad. The most intelligent person I know. My entire life, he's never answered my questions with "I don't know." Through peaks and valleys, he's always been there for me. He handles any situation, no matter how adverse, with such grace. Plus, he's extremely handsome!

–Andy Troy

When my dad came to this country at 16-years-old, his family didn't have much money and he didn't speak a word of English. Even though he was almost finished with school back in Sicily, he enrolled in high school as a freshman here in New Jersey. Four years later he went to college on a scholarship

and by the time he was 35, owne and operated two businesses th. he'd have for 30 years. Today, he a councilman in the town he live in. His story proves that we can o anything we set our minds to if w work hard, believe in ourselves an never give up!

–Joe Caramagn

And mine? Well I'm blesse with a lot, but I've got two amazin forces in my life—my mom an dad. They came here from Pakista in the `60s broke and alone. 5 years later they've helped mo people financially and emotional than I will probably ever know i my life. My mother texts me poem of love every day, and my dad, no diagnosed with cancer, still wake up every morning with a smile o his face and asks, "How are *you?"*

So with that, this issue i dedicated to all of the heroes in o lives—thanks for making us want t be the best version of ourselves.

Your turn, Carol Corps, fin someone to be an inspiration for.

Love, peace and spande>
San

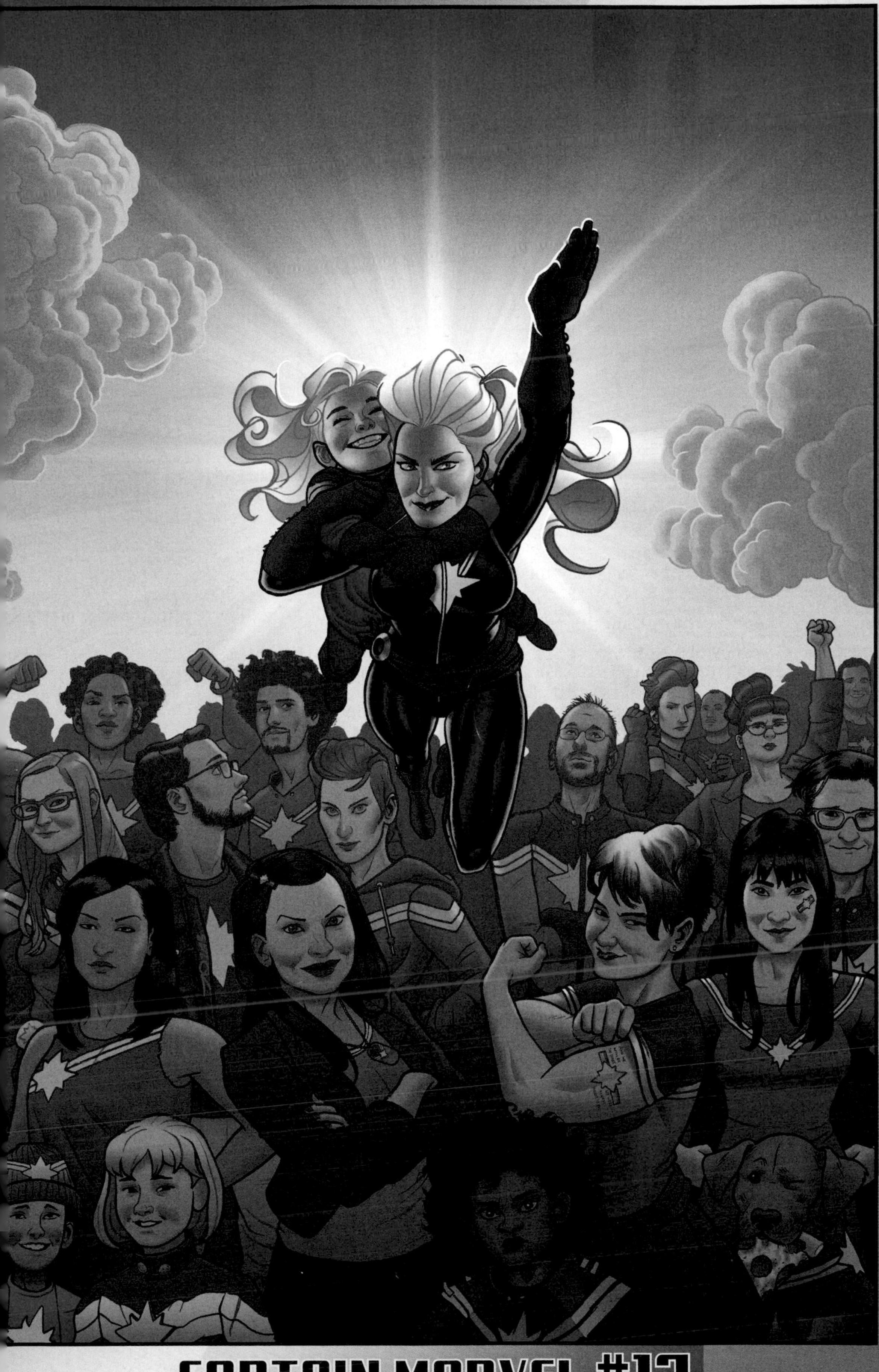

CAPTAIN MARVEL #17

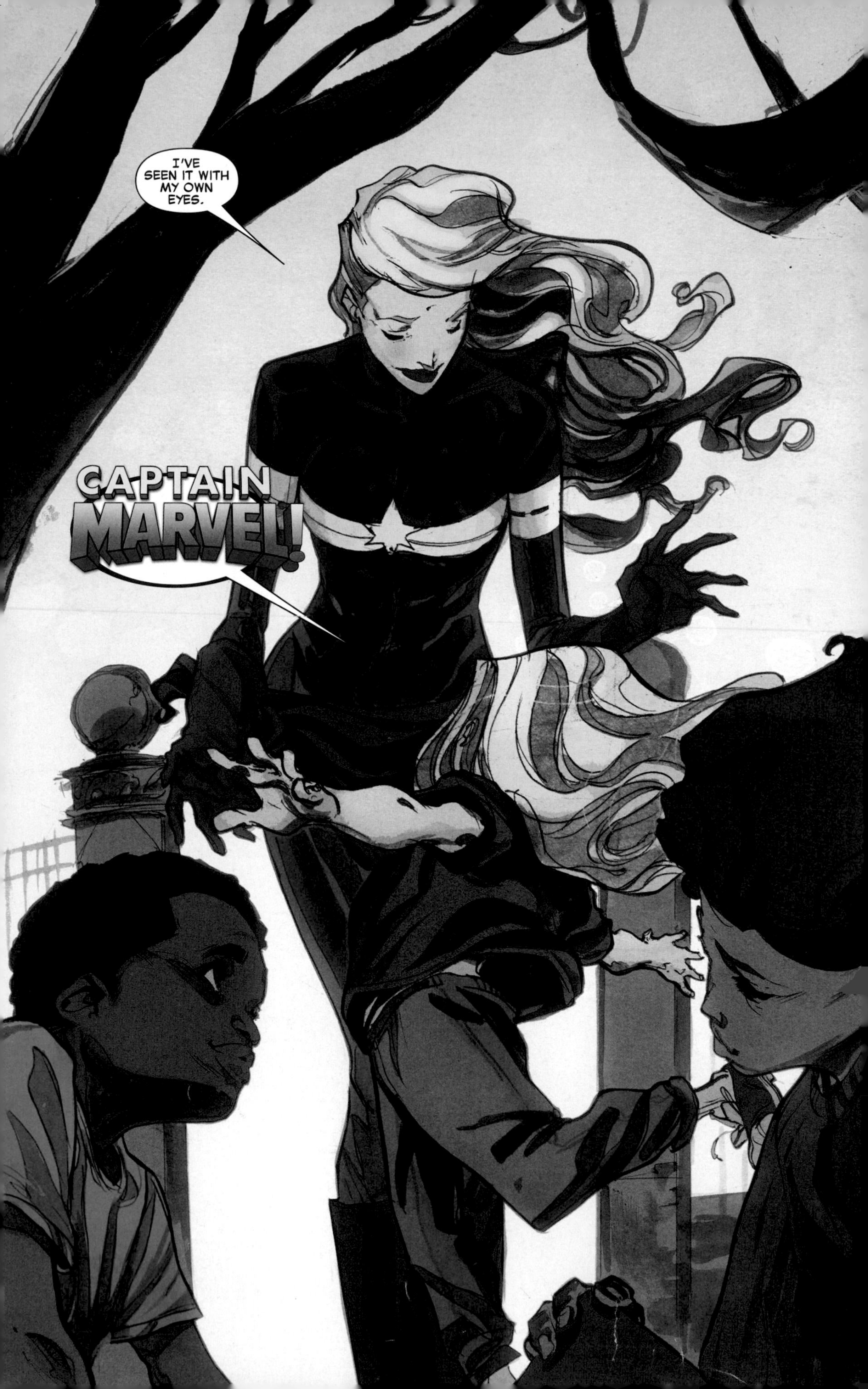
I'VE SEEN IT WITH MY OWN EYES.
CAPTAIN MARVEL!

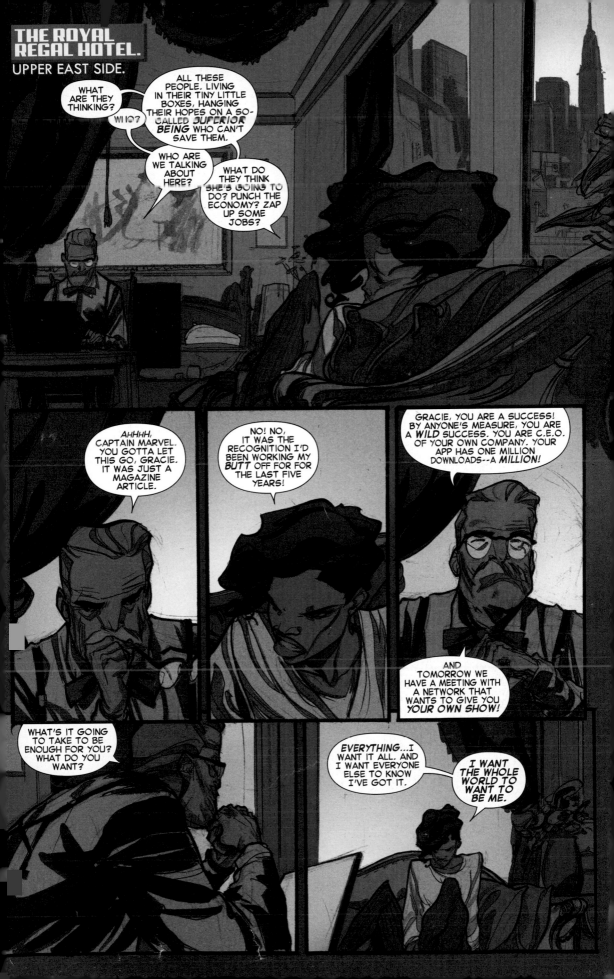

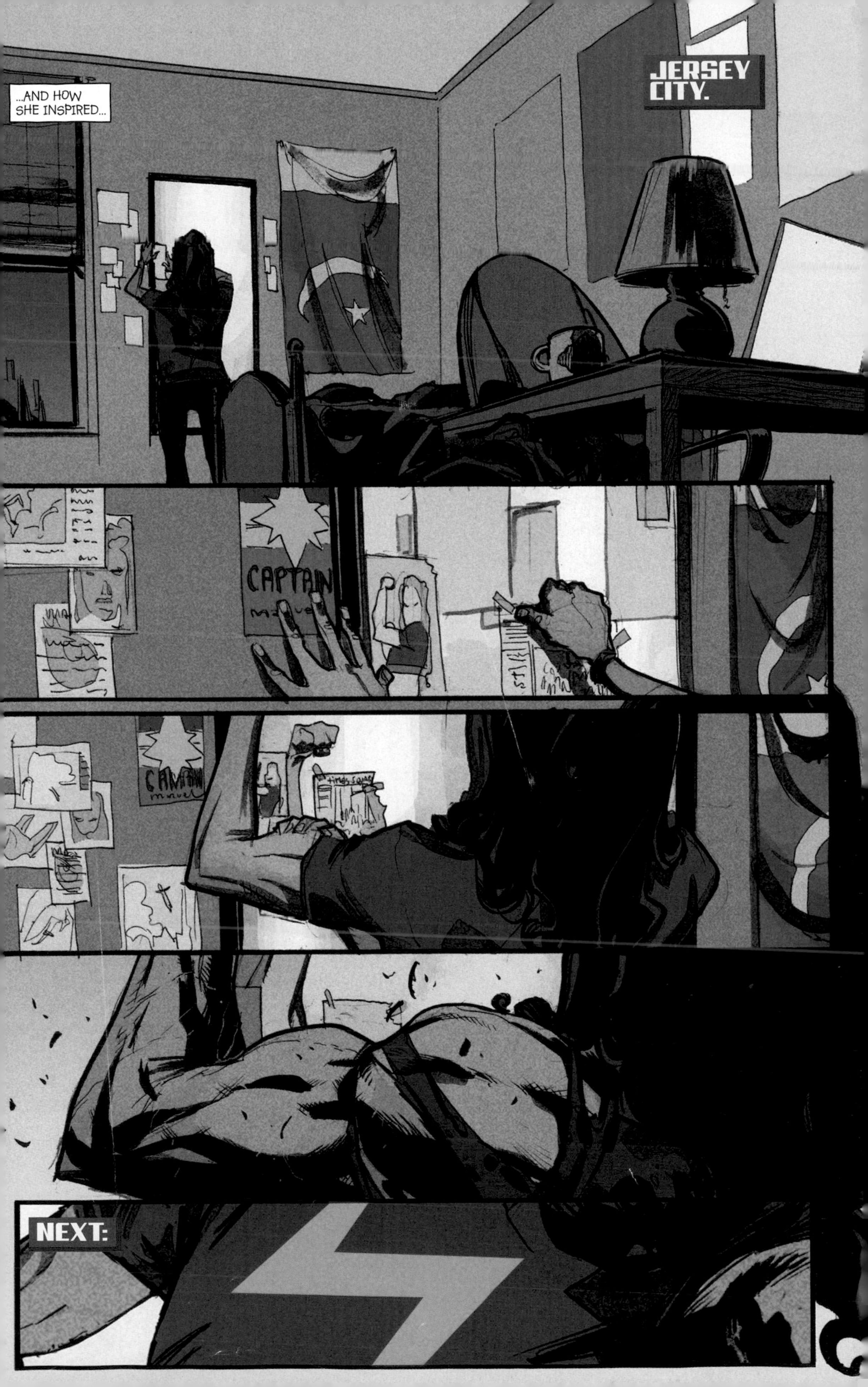

...AND HOW SHE INSPIRED...
JERSEY CITY.
CAPTAIN MARVEL
NEXT:

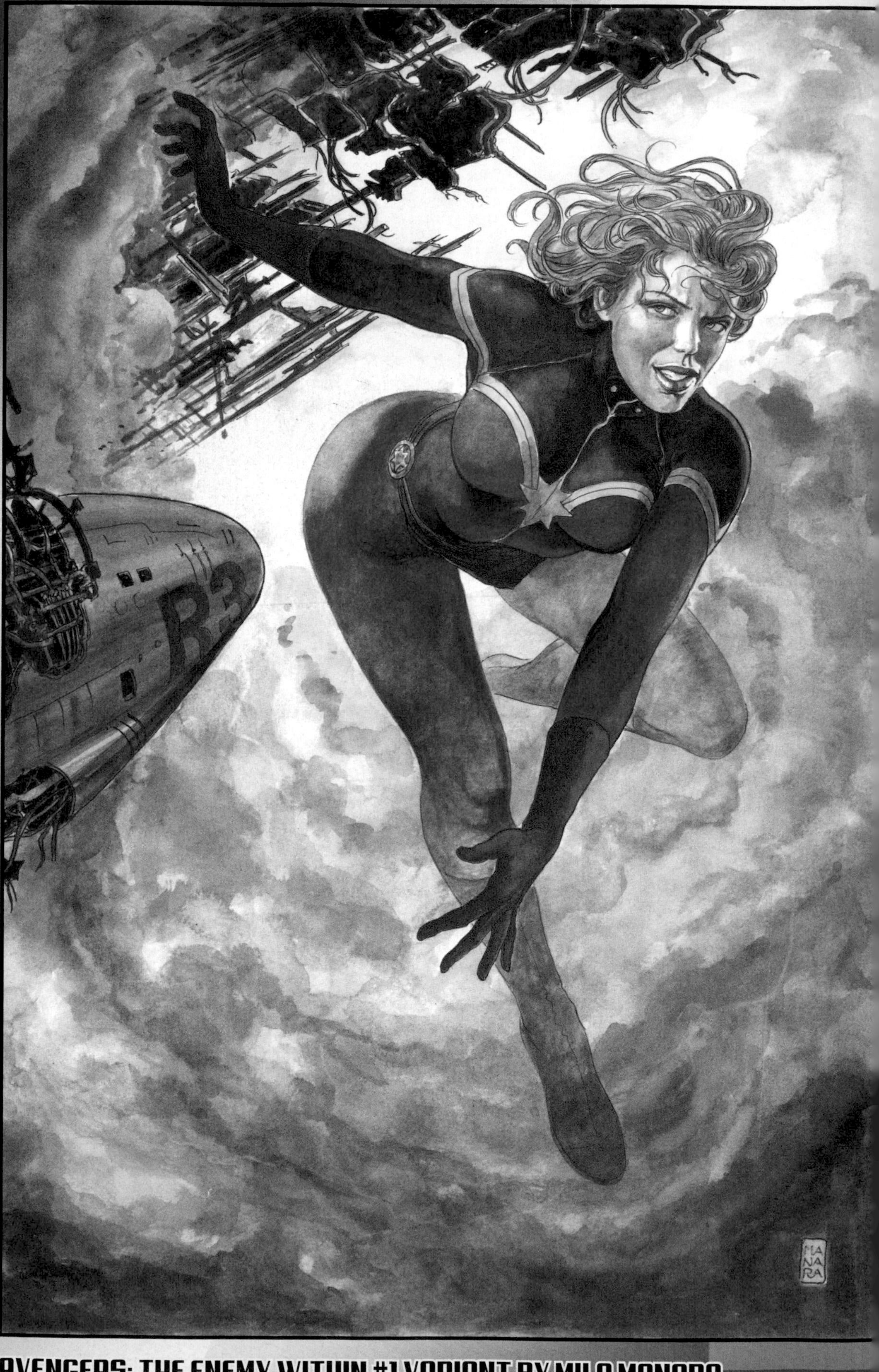
R3
MA
NA
RA

AVENGERS: THE ENEMY WITHIN #1 VARIANT BY MILO MANARA

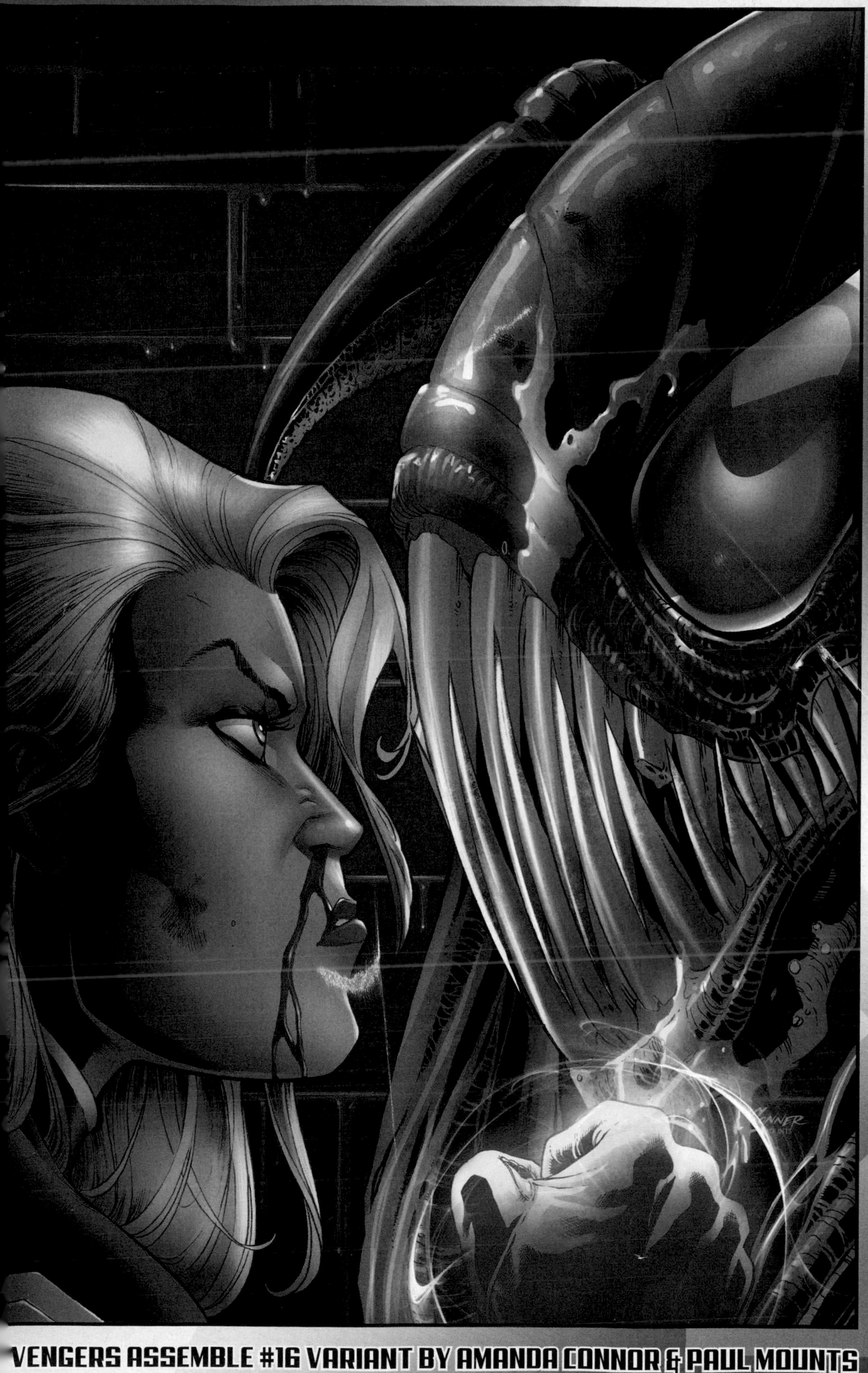

VENGERS ASSEMBLE #16 VARIANT BY AMANDA CONNOR & PAUL MOUNTS

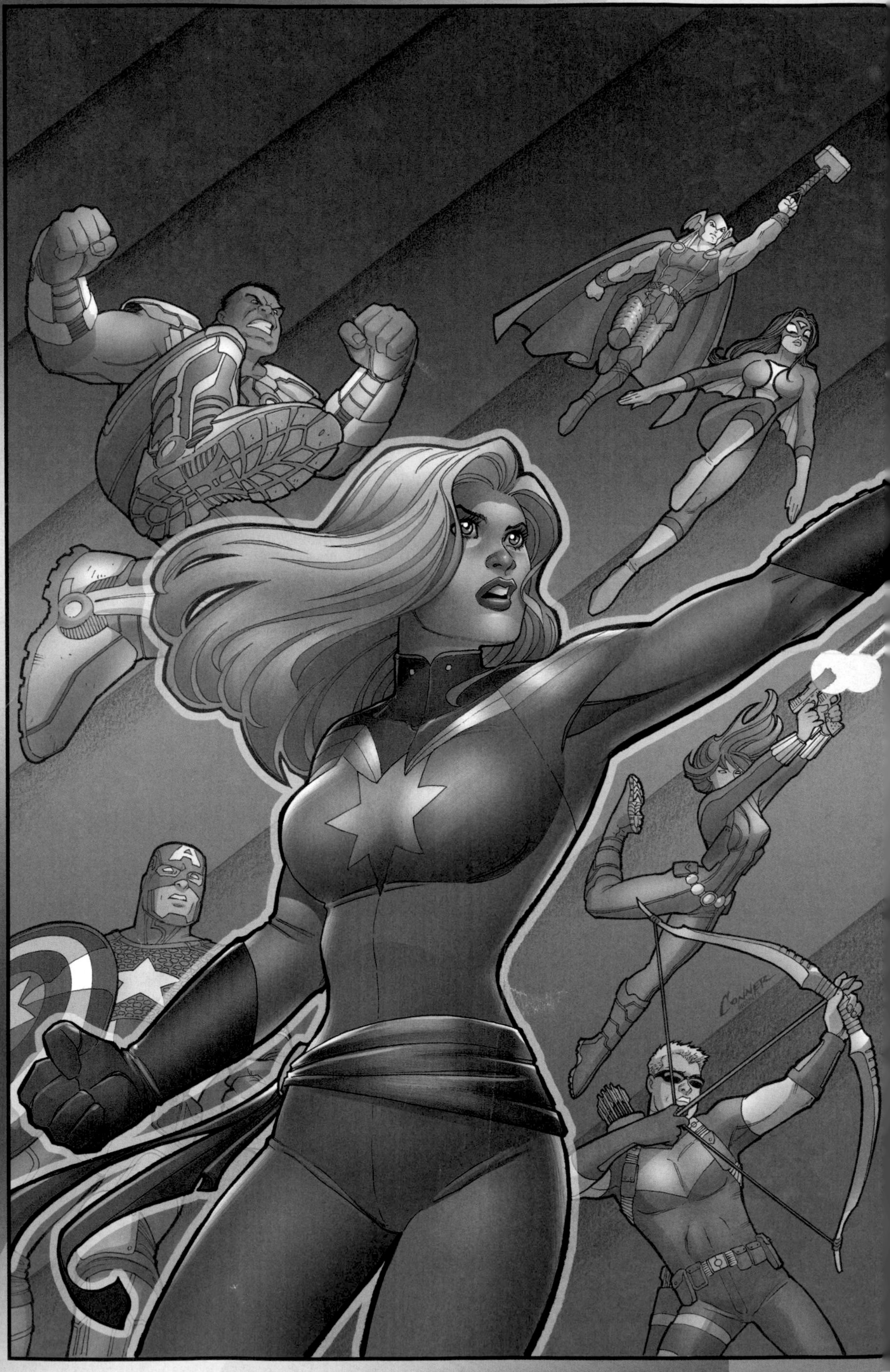

AVENGERS ASSEMBLE #17 VARIANT BY AMANDA CONNOR & PAUL MOUNT.

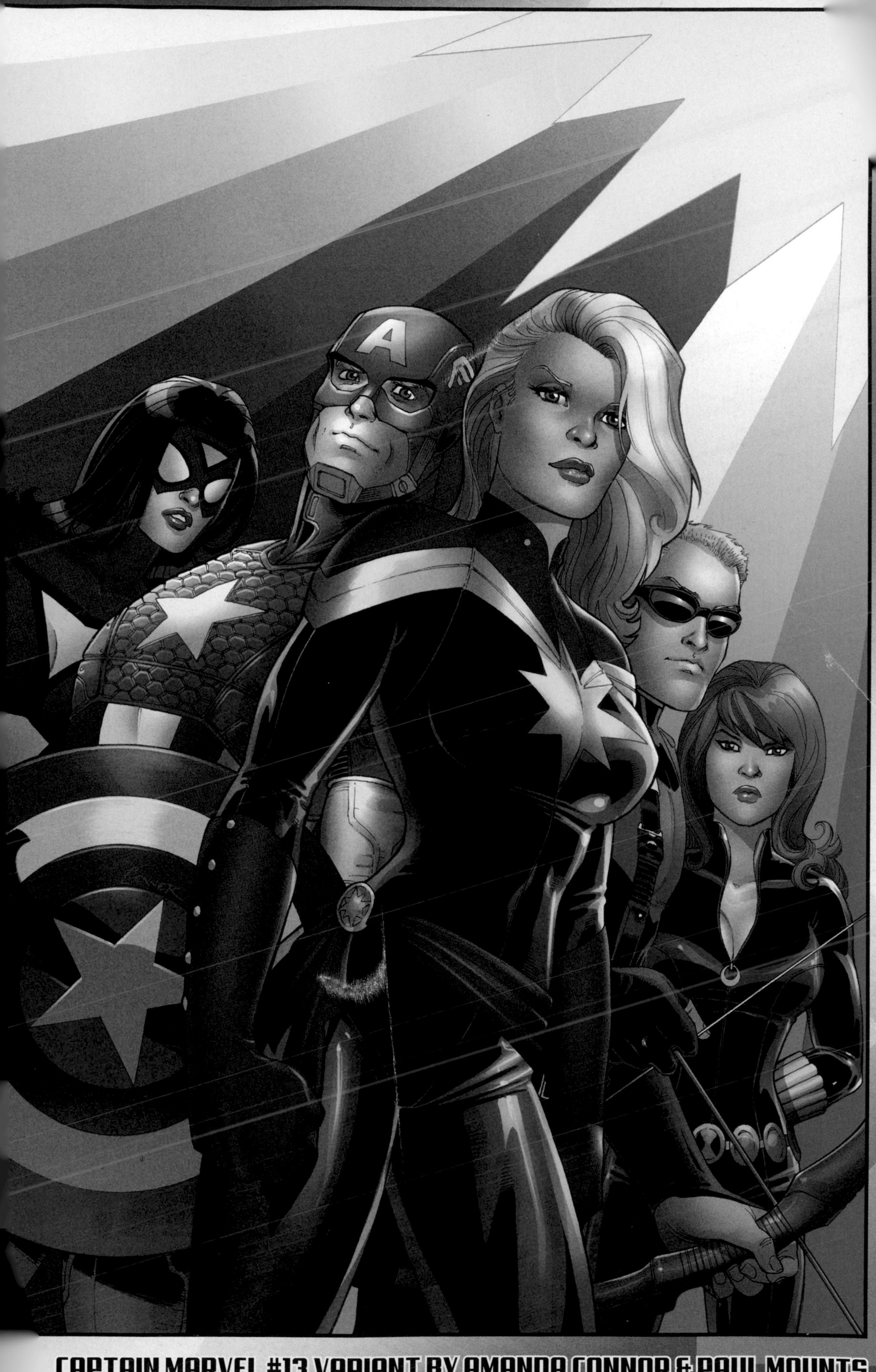

CAPTAIN MARVEL #13 VARIANT BY AMANDA CONNOR & PAUL MOUNTS

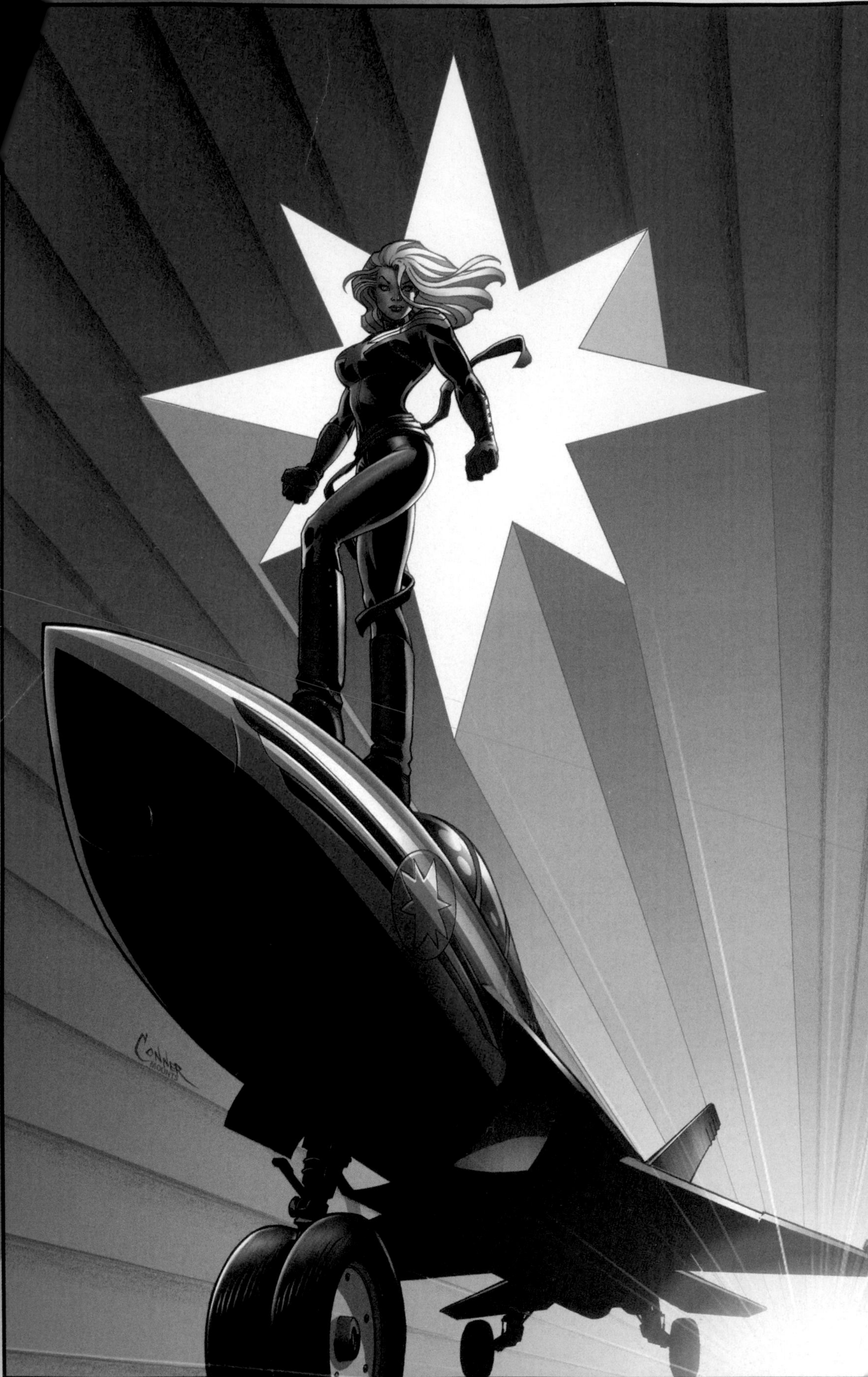

CAPTAIN MARVEL #14 VARIANT BY AMANDA CONNOR & PAUL MOUNTS

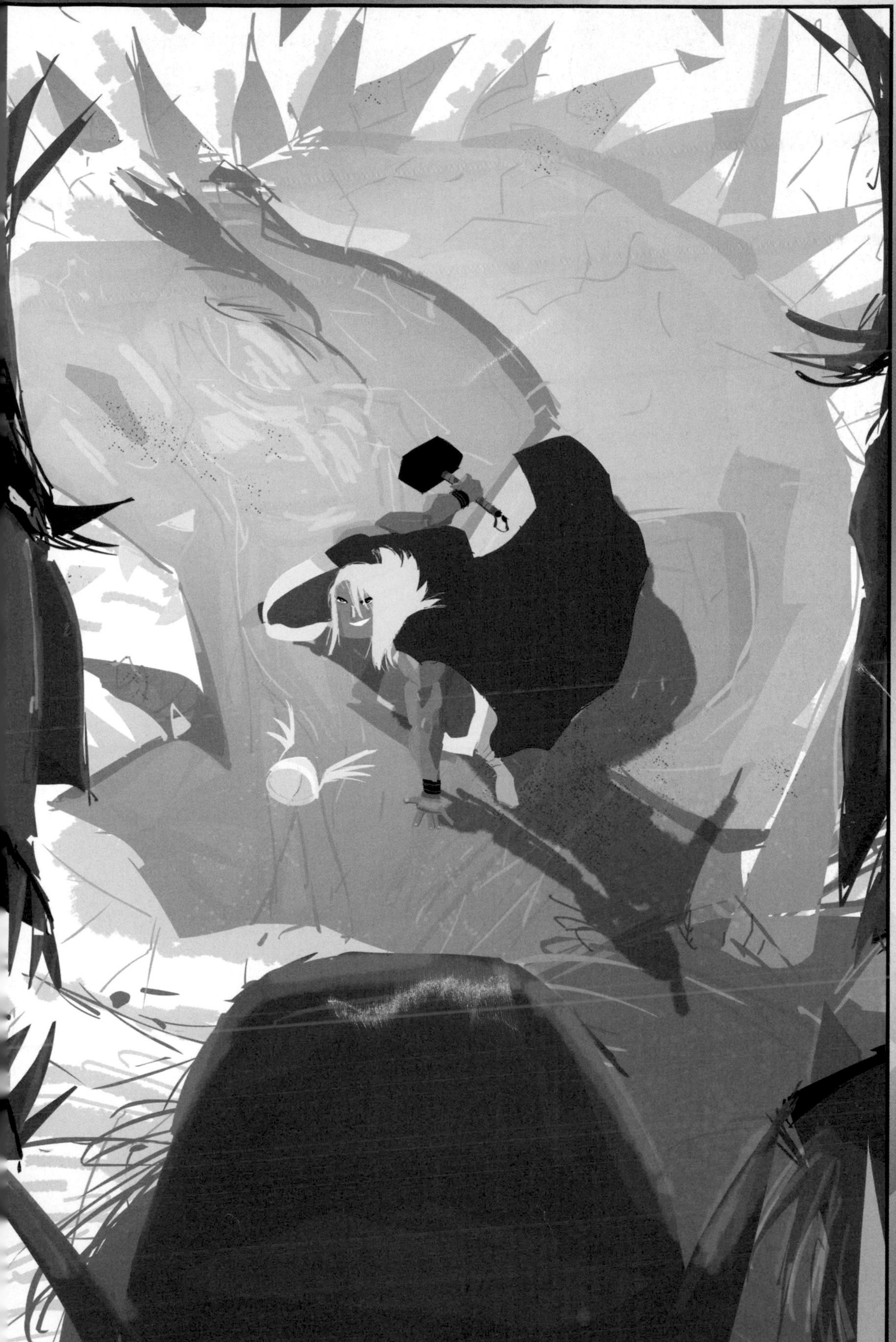

CAPTAIN MARVEL #17 THOR BATTLE VARIANT BY PASCAL CAMPION

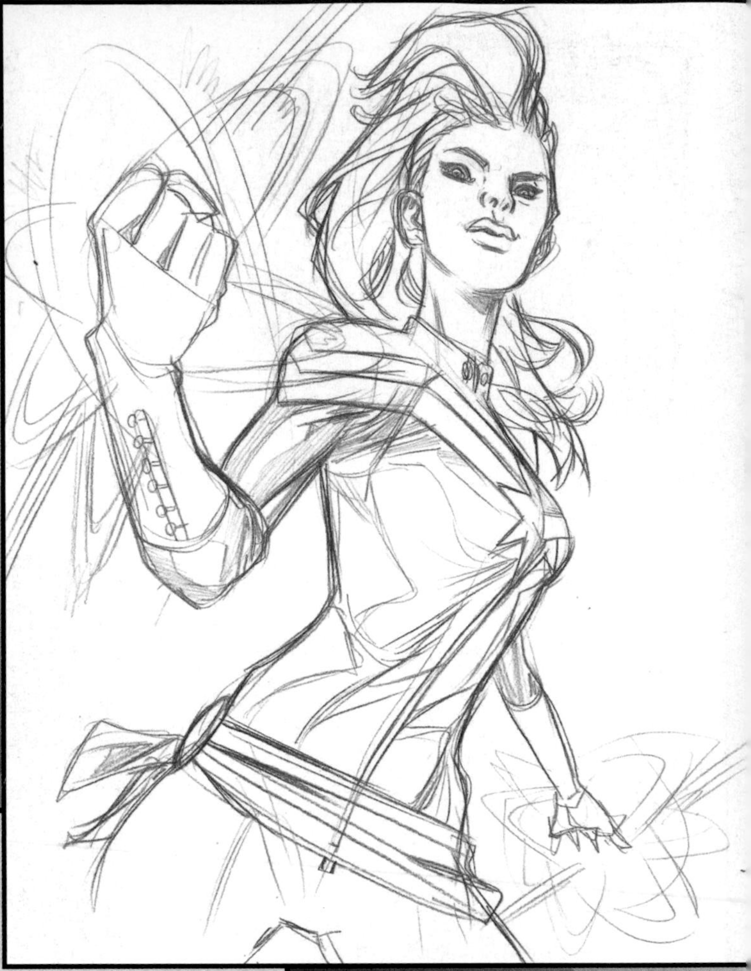

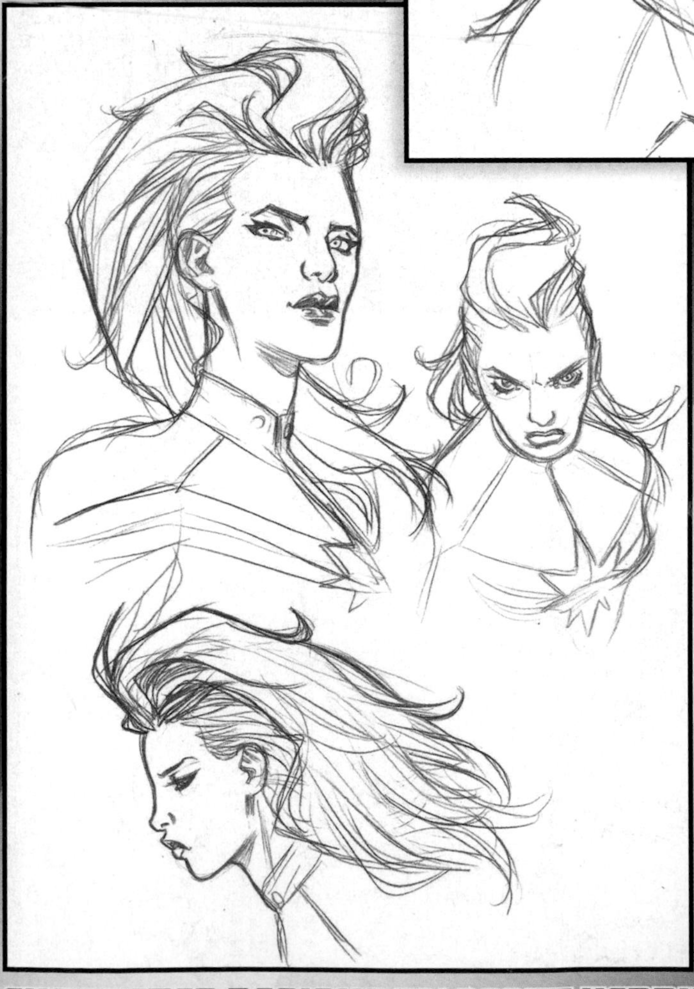

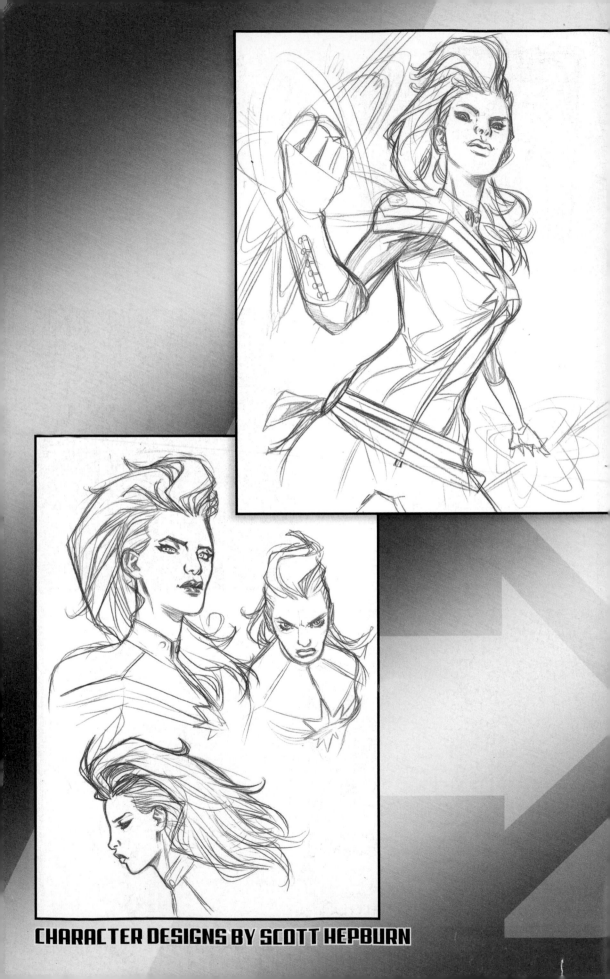

CHARACTER DESIGNS BY SCOTT HEPBURN